Monuments
Public Buildings
Educational Centres
Camino de Santiago
POLIGONO DOCENTE
C/. de Ernest Merimée
Francisco de Vitoria
Calle de Eloy García de Quevedo
Paseo Rintor
Centro Cívico RÍO VENA
PLAZA DE MARÍA CRUZ EBRO
Comandancia de Obras
PLAZA DE ANTONIO JOSÉ
PLAZA DE PEDRO MALDONADO
PLAZA DE MARÍA DE PACHECO
POLIGONO RÍO VENA
Calle de Juan Bravo
PLAZA DE FRAY JUSTO PÉREZ DE URBEL
Federación Comercio
Fernández
AVENIDA DE CANTABRIA
Palacio de Justicia
REYES CATÓLICOS
Paseo de los Comuneros de Castilla
Hogar de la Tercera Edad
Cultura Medio Ambiente
Calle de Juan de Padilla
Pasaderas
Policía Nacional Comisaría
Junta de Castilla y León
AVENIDA DE CASTILLA Y LEÓN
Calle de San Roque
Obdulio
Bartolomé Ordóñez
Carmen Sallés
San Nicolás
Calle Farmacéutico
PLAZA DE BILBAO
Manuel de la Cuesta
Avenida del Norte
Calle de Santo Domingo de Silos
Avenida de la Paz
Calle del Manzano
Virgen
Machado
Calle de Briviesca
Calzadas
Salamanca
Calle de las Calzadas
Jesús María Ordoño
Belorado
Calle de Cabezón
Delegación de Hacienda
Segovia
PLAZA DEL REY
Gobierno Militar
Justo del Río
CALLE DE VITORIA
Calle Alhucemas
Calle de Covadonga
PLAZA DE PAVÍA
Calle de Bailén
PLAZA NAVAS DE TOLOSA
C/. de Bailén
PLAZA DOS DE MAYO
Calle de la Cruz Roja
CRUZ ROJA
Estadio el Plantío
DEL RÍO ARLANZÓN
Paseo Regino Sáinz de la Maza
VITORIA
C/. de Ruiz
Sta. Casilda
Dorronsoro
AVENIDA
PARQUE DE LA QUINTA
PARQUE TEMÁTICO FORESTAL DE LA QUINTA
ARLANZÓN
Calle de la Cartuja de Miraflores
Calle Timoteo Arnaiz
Calle de San Pedro de Cardeña
Padre Diego Luis de San Vitores
Maestro Ricardo
Calle de Madre Calvo
Calle de San Pedro de Cardeña
Calle de Mateo Cerezo
Calle Diego de Siloé
Molinillo
Calle de Nicolás de Vergara
Obispo D. Mauricio
Calle de San José
Zatorre
Calle de las Casillas
Camino de Cortes
Cristóbal Andino
C/. de los Colonia
Crucero San Julián
Calle de Carcedo
S. JULIÁN
Parque del Crucero
Romanceros
Madrid - Irún

BURGOS
THE VISUAL GUIDE

Subsidized edition

Junta de
Castilla y León
Consejería de Cultura y Turismo

Title BURGOS, The Visual Guide

© Script and texts on History and Art History LUIS MARTÍNEZ GARCÍA
Professor of Medieval History, University of Burgos
RENÉ J. PAYO HERRANZ
Professor of Art History, University of Burgos

© Photographs HERRÁIZ Fotógrafos
With the photographic collaboration of Belén García, Luis Mena, Antonio Gutiérrez and Carlos Calleja

© Back cover maps and 3D graphs RASA ESTUDIO

© Drawings and inside maps CUADRADO DISEÑO

© This edition AYUNTAMIENTO DE BURGOS

Layout CUADRADO DISEÑO, RICO ADRADOS, RAMÓN SÁNCHEZ AND TEXT AUTHORS.

Photosetting RICO ADRADOS, S.L.

Printing GRAFICAS CASTILLA

Translation TWOBE, S.L.

Acknowledgements Cabildo Metropolitano de la Catedral de Burgos, Patronato de los Reales Monasterios, Patrimonio Nacional, Federación de Empresarios de Comercio de Burgos, Fundación Atapuerca, Museo de Burgos, Mauricio Antón

I.S.B.N.: 978-84-87876-16-5
NATIONAL BOOK CATALOGUE NUMBER: BU-49. – 2007
Printed in Burgos

BURGOS
THE VISUAL GUIDE

City history

■ Location

Today Burgos is a historical city with an eye on the future; it preserves its past and, at the same time, pays attention to the growth of the present. A plural and modern city with a population of 166,000, Burgos is the second largest metropolis and the industrial engine of the Comunidad Autónoma de Castilla y León (Autonomous Region of Castilla y León). It is the capital and geographical centre of an extraordinarily attractive province, a rich compendium of history, art, nature and cuisine, with a university of 11,000 students and a wide variety of cultural activities.

Burgos has always enjoyed a privileged geographical location, acting as an intermediary between the northern and southern halves of the country and, due to the Camino de Santiago pilgrim route, also between the east and the west. Today, Burgos is an important hub in the national road network –it is crossed by the northern highway and its eastern diversion, as

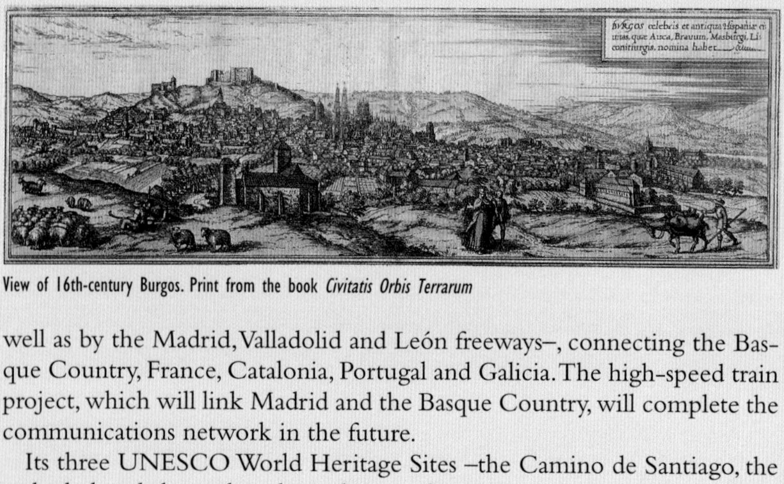

View of 16th-century Burgos. Print from the book *Civitatis Orbis Terrarum*

well as by the Madrid, Valladolid and León freeways–, connecting the Basque Country, France, Catalonia, Portugal and Galicia. The high-speed train project, which will link Madrid and the Basque Country, will complete the communications network in the future.

Its three UNESCO World Heritage Sites –the Camino de Santiago, the cathedral and the archaeological sites of Atapuerca, the birthplace of the earliest European settlers– confirm its crucial historical role as a cultural crossroads.

■ Historical evolution of the city

The origins

Burgos means *fortified enclosure*, and that is precisely what it was originally. Burgos came into being in 884 AC, on the Cerro de San Miguel, when the Count Diego Porcelos decided to populate the area and establish a military fortress under the Asturian king Alfonso III. Evidence of Neolithic human settlements (4,500 years BC) and irrefutable remains of the Eneolithic period (2,500 years BC) and of the Early Iron Age (850 BC) have been found on the top of that hill.

In the beginning, Burgos was a mere link in the chain of Christian fortresses erected in the Castilian territories, such as Amaya, Castrojeriz, Cerezo or Clunia. But by the year 1000, the defensive military fortress had al-

ready become a vigorous town expanding downhill towards the bank of the river Arlanzón. Documents of the 10th century describe the farming and commercial activities of the town. Mention is also made to the existence of some suburbs such as San Juan, to the east, and San Pedro de Eras, to the west.

Simultaneously, Burgos became the political and administrative centre of a small region, the so-called *alfoz*, and of the county of Castile. In 915 it achieved city status and in 932, under Fernán González, it became the main city in Castile; not surprisingly, considering its central location, equidistant from the Bay of Biscay, the rivers Duero and Pisuerga, and the border of Navarra.

The origins of Castile. Mural painting by Vela Zanetti, Arco de Santa María

The Middle Ages

During the 11th and 13th centuries Burgos achieved the maturity that was to be expected of a medieval town. The signs of such maturity were: urban compactness, commercial and craft activities, institutional development and cultural renovation.

The 11th century was a century of awakening in Europe, and Burgos felt the effects of this awakening. On the one hand, these lands were not borderlands any longer, which encouraged the area's demographic and economic development. The names of the new city quarters find their way into the official documents of the time, in relation with peripheral churches such as San Esteban, San Llorente, San Román or San Martín and, a little later, Nuestra Señora de Viejarrúa, San Nicolás, Santa Agueda, Santiago and San Gil. All of these quarters stood on the foothill, keeping very much to themselves, politically dependent on the castle, but with an enormous economic potential.

On the other hand, the city had become the habitual place of residence of the early Castilian kings (Fernando I, 1037) and of the notable members of the aristocracy, who settled down in the city allured by generous fiscal privileges.

But, in addition to the above, other significant events took place during the Middle Ages, such as the establishment of the Episcopal headquarters (which moved from Oca to Burgos in 1075) and, more importantly, the growing popularity of the Camino

Catedral and Arco de Santa María. 19th-century lithograph

de Santiago, due to the European political orientation of Alfonso VI. Burgos was soon to become one of the main stops along the Camino. Through the Camino came foreign products and ideas, brought in by the French, the Jews or the Mozarabs, who gradually settled in the new quarters and other suburbs such as Santa María –where the original cathedral was erected–, La Llana, Huerto del Rey or La Vega. The first hospitals for pilgrims were built in 1085 at the request of the king: the Hospital de San Juan and the Hospital del Emperador, at the entrance and exit of the city, respectively. Also, Saint Lesmes settled down in the area with a number of French monks from the abbey of Casa Dei, ambassadors of the European culture of the time.

During the 12th and 13th centuries the demographic growth and the diversification of the economic activities sped up significantly. By the end of that period the population had reached 7,000. At the same time, profound specialisation processes were taking place within the traditional trades –blacksmiths, furriers, carpenters, weavers or money changers– and Burgos' commercial activity experienced an unprecedented growth, achieving international dimensions due to the Castilian conquests in the south of the peninsula and to the city's new role as a top distribution centre.

Capilla de la Asunción, Monasterio de las Huelgas. 19th-century lithograph

This economic complexity had an impact on the city's social structure. In addition to the traditional farmers and market gardeners, new social groups came into existence, rigidly structured and well defined according to their economic activity or their ethnic and religious background. Craftsmen and merchants, Moors and Jews, gave the city a new flair. Social differences deepened, until a clear line was drawn between the urban oligarchy, mostly of foreign background (Ramón Bonifaz, Guiralt Almeric, Arnalt de Sanchester...), linked to the commercial activities and well integrated in the city's chivalry, and the rest of the population, formed by craftsmen, farmers, the poor and the underprivileged. Very soon the former would impose their economic predominance and their social prestige in order to gain access to the different posts of the city council.

This new economic and social reality called for new ways of political organisation, different from the traditional ones linked to the castle and the bishopric, the two other local powers. Throughout the 12th and 13th centuries the Burgos council obtained from the Crown a series of privileges and competencies. The more their privileges grew, the more the popular layers of society were neglected. The council not only exercised its power within the city walls, but it also became the administrative centre of a vast

territory and the owner of feudal lands that included strategic castles and villages such as Lara and its surrounding area, Barbadillo del Mercado, Pampliega, Pancorbo o Miranda de Ebro.

This progress had an impact on the land occupation methods. The castle lost part of its former power. The population became more compact, and tended to concentrate in the lower areas of the city, preferably along Calle Tenebregosa and Calle Viejarrúa (today's Calle Fernán González) –used by the pilgrims of the Camino de Santiago and home to most of the shops and newly-erected churches– and around the quarters of Santa María and Las Llanas, thus blending the old quarters together. By the end of the 12th century, the southern border of the city was the river Vena: from the Pellejería de San Gil and across the Huerto del Rey and Las Llanas, skirting the old cathedral of Alfonso VI. A few years later, in the early 13th century, a new cathedral was erected and a new wall was built –the ones standing today–, which defined and consolidated the urban landscape. Meanwhile, on the other side of the river, outside the wall, the Vega quarter took shape, thanks to the construction, at the end of the 12th century, of the royal residential complex of Las Huelgas and the Puebla de San Felices, financed by the monastery.

Crossed daily by hundreds of pilgrims, under the control of clergymen and merchants, Burgos had become directly intertwined with European culture. The elite imposed its tastes. Throughout the city sprang altars and chapels dedicated to the apostle Santiago (Saint James), built in the Romanesque or French Gothic styles by local architects and Mudéjar stonemasons, and the shops sold surplus products from the fields and the craft activities.

The Late Middle Ages

The 14th century was one of recession in Burgos, in Castile, and in Europe in general. The commercial circuits collapsed due to the lack of surplus farming products; the higher classes became more and more violent, particularly the laymen, bent on maintaining at all costs the level of their rents; a civil war broke out between Pedro I and Enrique of Trastámara; and ethnic minorities started to be persecuted. The leading groups reinforced their political power by means of the so-called Regimiento, a ruling system established by Alfonso XI in 1345.

Something similar happened in the culture department. The city's monumental projects had by then been finished, and all that was left to do was make additions or carry out renovations, at the initiative of the Church, as it was the case with the cloister of the cathedral or the churches of San Gil and San Esteban.

The 15th century brought along a process of recovery, mainly during its second half, which continued during the first half of the following century. It was the

Sunrise in Burgos

heyday of the city by the Arlanzón. Population doubled, reaching 14,000. Commerce was instrumental to the recovery, international commerce in particular, of which Burgos became the undisputed capital. Several factors contributed to this: the scarcity of local natural resources, the expansion of sheep raising, the Camino de Santiago, the proximity of the ports of the Bay of Biscay, and the take-off of commercial relations between the north and the south of Europe after the blockage on wool exports imposed by England onto the industrial centres of Flanders.

Internally, the city maintained its craft industry and a commerce aimed at securing internal supplies. There was a daily market, plus a weekly market and an annual 15-day fair in June, starting on Saint John's day. All of them, however, depended on the needs of the big merchants. The whole city revolved around them, attentive to their business transactions, which sustained it to a large extent.

Arco de Santa María. Drawing by Isidro Gil

The merchants of Burgos gained control of the commercial traffic of the European Atlantic shores, creating a thick network of colonies, agents and companies, distributed all over the continent, mainly in the region of Flanders, where two cities –Bruges and then Antwerp– became particularly active.

The main export product was wool. Other important products were iron from Biscay, oil, wine, salt, fruit, fabrics of different qualities, alum, etc.

Everything was strictly regulated. As early as the 13th century, the merchants of Burgos had grouped in guilds in order to protect themselves from potential competitors. The Universidad de Mercaderes (University of Merchants) was funded in 1455, with a number of schools abroad, enjoying special privileges, and in 1494 the Catholic Monarchs established the Consulado del Mar (Consulate of the Sea), which meant the creation of a jurisdiction with legal competences on commercial affairs, similar to Valencia and Barcelona.

Paradoxically, the big merchants of Burgos, organised in domestic enterprises, well coordinated, familiar with the newest methods of payment and credit, and owners of large fortunes, ended up emulating the feudal aristocracy, purchasing land and acquiring mansions, palaces and castles in the city and its surrounding area. Their economic vigour and the admiration they felt for the humanist culture, with which they became acquainted through their commercial contacts with Flanders and Italy, would foster the patronage of craftsmen and the promotion of numerous artistic manifestations.

This process was pioneered by Alonso de Cartagena, who brought to Burgos the master Juan de Colonia in order to build the spires and the dome of the cathedral, which was accomplished between 1442 and 1445. Many other works were carried out following on Juan de Colonia's steps, mostly by advanced disciples, including a profusion of chapels and tombs, in the cathedral, in the monasteries, and in most of the fifteen urban parochial churches.

As to urban design, most of the construction activity concentrated in the cathedral area and in the eastern section of the *intramuros* (within walls) city, in the San Juan quarter. Meanwhile, the higher quarters became gradually devaluated and were occupied by the lower classes and the socially excluded groups, such as the Jews and de Mudéjares. Their situation worsened drastically with the triumph of queen Isabel in the War of Succession, which ended in 1475, when the castle –whose lord, Íñigo de Stúñiga, had supported Juana la Beltraneja and participated in the massive destruction of streets and houses– was taken. The subsequent persecution of the minorities, in order to achieve religious unity, further degraded the area.

Modern Times

The 16th century is of particular relevance to the history of Burgos. It saw the city's economic heyday and the beginning of its decline. The city was in the hands of an oligarchy formed by the members of the small nobility and, above all, by big merchants, some of them converts, whose mind was open to the new cultural currents coming from abroad, and who held municipal power in close collaboration with the Crown. Their names were Sarmiento, Melgosa, Bernuy, Angulo, Maluenda, Quintanadueñas, etc.

Emblem of the Consulado del Mar, Academia de Dibujo

During the comunero uprising in Burgos, the city patricians adopted moderate positions prior to leaving the Comunidades. A few years later they made clear their loyalty to the king by building the façade of the Puerta de Santa María in honour of Carlos I. The oligarchy had stood out against the pretensions of the popular sector, which demanded a greater participation in the institutions.

The external image of the city was hardly altered. The walls continued to mark the difference with the countryside, although the gates were now constantly crossed by wealthy merchants like Miranda, Íñigo Angulo and the Melgosas, who had built their estates on the other side of the river Arlanzón, next to the Vega quarter, as the higher quarters of the city were gradually abandoned.

As to the art scene, the 16th experienced a great creative development. The Gothic style reached its climax and then gave way to a profusion of Renaissance monuments, both ecclesiastical and civil. The Capilla del Condestable, in the cathedral, and the cathedral's dome are two examples of this architectural evolution. The art of sculpture reached spectacular levels, both in terms of quantity and quality. Artists like Felipe Vigarny, Diego de Siloe or Domingo de Amberes, among others, turned the so-called Burgos

School into a national point of reference. This is the Plateresque period. The church portals, altarpieces, tombs and funereal chapels were gradually covered with images and scenes filled with realism and beauty. The clergy still led the cultural activity of the time, and many clergymen, such as Pedro de Lerma, co-founder, together with Cisneros, of the University of Alcalá de Henares, or Francisco de Encinas, closely watched by the Holy Inquisition, were in favour of the Erasmist humanism that had spread all over Europe. Other important personalities of the time were brother Francisco de Vitoria, who wrote the Leyes de Burgos (Burgos Law) of 1512, or the archdeacon Pedro Fernández de Villegas, translator of the *Divine Comedy*.

In the second half of the century, the commercial splendour of Burgos started to decline drastically, which affected the whole city.

17th-century view of Burgos. Print by M. Merian

Several factors account for this decline. One of the reasons is that the Burgos merchants never bothered to set up a solid and diversified economic structure in the city. They hardly showed any interest in promoting the craft industry or in intensifying the farming production, but made investments in the countryside with a view to gaining prestige, following updated criteria of a feudal nature. They were happy to be mere intermediaries and to carry goods from one place to another, without a stable foundation and without involving the working population in their businesses.

There were other reasons. The first difficulties started in Flanders, during the middle years of the century, when the demand for textile products decreased. The situation worsened due to the increase of piracy, the upraising of the Flemish Protestants, the capture of the Castilian fleet in Middleburg in 1574, and the destruction of Antwerp a year later. The heavy debt of the treasury of Felipe II caused not only the bankruptcy of those involved in the fair of Medina del Campo, but also the increase of fiscal pressure and the removal of the Court to Madrid, which shifted the economic and political centre of the country from Castile to the other side of the Cordillera Central mountain range.

During the 17th century and most of the 18th, Burgos suffered a profound decline. Population dwindled from 12,000 at the end of the 16th century to a bit over 6,000 in 1631, due to the generalised epidemics and hunger, to the emigration of rural people, and to the deterioration of the living conditions due to the lack of work. A certain degree of recovery was felt at the turn of the century, with the population reaching 9,000, thanks to the improvement of the economic situation.

The demographic descent had a negative impact on the craft industry, which had always been in a weaker position, and also on the wool trade, which virtually disappeared. However, rural activity was intensified in the

farming area that surrounded the city and in some spaces within the city walls, which had been abandoned after the population recession.

The social structure then consisted of a large population of clergymen and hidalgos, with more or less fortune, plus many poor, a small number of craftsmen and merchants unable to meet the needs of the powerful, a slightly larger number of civil servants and professionals, who lived better than most, and, on the top of the social pyramid, around 60 families who dominated the political scene –they occupied the most important posts of the Regimiento– and enjoyed the support of the clergy, without a doubt the most influential social group.

Those were times of urban and artistic recession, compared to the vigorous activity of the previous century. However, there was some activity connected with the Classical and Baroque altarpieces of many churches –particularly the cathedral, where activity never stopped–, as well as with works of funereal sculpture.

La Llana marketplace. Lithograph by G. Doré

By the end of this period, and coinciding with the beginning of the Enlightenment, there was a new recovery. The Consulado was reborn in 1766, with a view to managing as a monopoly, as it had been done in the past, the trading of Castilian wool. Around the Consulado thrived a group of entrepreneurs determined to modernise the city by improving its communications, mainly with the northern section of the country, reactivating the economy, and improving the education system and the city's image.

Their activities left a clear mark on the city map. The statue of the king Carlos III (1784), located in today's Plaza Mayor, symbolically acknowledged a series of initiatives that led to the building of the Casa Consistorial (City Hall), on the land left vacant after pulling down the walls in 1772, and to the construction of a large pedestrian area, the Paseo del Espolón, which marked the beginning of a new era of expansion, beyond the walled-in city, leaving behind the medieval city.

The 19th Century

The 19th century was a time of modernisation in Burgos. The city took advantage of the vigour of the Enlightenment and the stimulating effects of the sale of the Church lands, of its condition as administrative and services centre, and of the construction of the road and railroad net-

Aerial view of Burgos. Lithograph by A. Guesdon (1851)

works. The population tripled, the economy took off, and the social structure became more complex. A new bourgeois social elite gained access to the political power. All these changes had an impact on the city structure, originally medieval, which went through a deep transformation process.

The conversion of a rural and farming society into a modern, industrial one was, however, very slow. Many archaic elements were still present in the early 19th century. The castle and the belfries of the churches and convents still dominated the compact urban structure. The land continued to be the main source of wealth, a sign of social distinction for the upper classes of the Old Regime. Commerce was still meagre, kept alive by the intermittent fairs and markets. Industrial activity was mostly domestic. The Church imposed the norms of public conduct and morals, and artists took inspiration from the past, particularly from the revered medieval period and its heroes.

BATAILLE ET PRISE DE BURGOS

The Battle of Burgos during the War of Independence (1808)

The century began with the War of Independence. The French occupation had a deep impact on the life of the city. Occupied from 1808 until 1813, as a strategic enclave on the road to Madrid and Portugal, the city had to suffer the presence of the French troops, which demanded food and unscrupulously took up the city's most emblematic edifices, and, later on, the Spanish ones. Finally, the withdrawal of the French army was accompanied by the blowing up of the castle, which caused serious damages to the surrounding buildings. Then the city became self-absorbed, in search of its old, updated signs of identity. Fortunately, it found none.

After the Absolutist Decade (1823-1833), a new cycle started, which, in general terms, lasted until the 1960's. It was then that the modern city was born, the bourgeois city, adapted to the new social and economic life of the industrial capitalism and the liberal bourgeoisie. And if it did not reach the same level of development as other Spanish cities, it was due to the lack of initiative of the social groups linked to the ecclesiastical and military nobility. But there were groups of merchants, professionals and civil servants who were bent on making changes. This is what they achieved:

- The population grew thanks to the constant influx of immigrants from the country. It was 10,000 at the beginning of the century, and reached 30,000 a hundred years later.
- The new elites took advantage of the sales of the Church lands and purchased land and real estate properties, until then in the hands of the ecclesiastical institutions. In the late 19th century, the number of owners had tripled and the land was owned by tenants, professionals, craftsmen and small merchants, that is, by the bourgeoisie and the middle classes, who also controlled the municipal and provincial institutions.

- The city benefited from the administrative reorganisation of the liberal State, which involved the creation of the provincial capital status and the concentration of legal, health, educational, religious and military services, which filled the city with civil servants and professionals and, also, with public edifices such as the Audiencia Territorial or the Diputación Provincial.
- Due to its geographic situation, Burgos felt very soon the effects of the modernisation of the communications. The northern railroad, which linked Madrid and France, started operating in 1860, and the first private automobile ran through the city streets in 1900.

As all this happened, the new bourgeoisie gradually built a city to suit its own needs, the historical city that we know today, respecting the medieval framework, without expanding nor building new large suburbs, but pulling down the walls, covering or diverting the water channels and widening the streets.

Romantic image of Burgos. Lithograph by R. de Launay (1813)

Urban renovation efforts concentrated in the flat areas of the old city, around the market squares and the adjacent streets –Paloma, Laín Calvo, San Juan, La Puebla–. The houses of the powerful families were built there; also the large public buildings and the broad promenades, where the bourgeoisie mingled and showed off their power, mainly at the Espolón, with its casinos, the Teatro Principal and the cafés. The houses were completely refurbished; the empty lots and old orchards were built up, new three-storey buildings sprang up all over the city, and house fronts were filled with large windows and balconies.

Meanwhile, the upper areas of the castle hill, to which the bourgeoisie did not relate any longer, deteriorated both physically and socially, and the southern area, on the other side of the river Arlanzón, received the influx of working immigrants and was built up with poor structures lacking infrastructure, a reflection of the existing social differences.

During the last quarter of the century, the city centre being saturated and fully renovated, a new exclusive residential area was created by the bourgeoisie in the Paseo de la Isla. The Real Audiencia and a branch of the Banco de España were built there, as well as several private palaces.

The 20th Century

At the beginning of the 20th century Burgos looked like a modern and renovated city, but was still weighed down by the mistakes of the past. The heaviest ballast was economical. Agriculture remained the main source of wealth for the upper classes. Industry did not manage to take off, and the most ambitious projects of the time, such as the Fábrica de Tabaco (Tobacco Factory), in 1888, and the Sociedad Azucarera Burgalesa (Burgos Sugar

Society), in 1900, failed. Commerce was that of a modest, well-communicated, service city, so the hotel business flourished and new hotels were built, such as the Gran Hotel de París, the Norte y Londres and the Universal. The authorities and the press started to demand the renovation of the road and railroad infrastructure: this was to bring about deep changes in the north-south communications within the province, which not always turned out to be beneficial to the capital.

Plaza Mayor. Photograph by Laurent (1872)

From the social point of view, differences were still deep. Most of the population lived below the poverty threshold, especially when the harvest was poor. The changes of the 19th century had benefited a select minority with a tenant mentality, with little economic and political impact at a national level but highly regarded locally. These elites promoted the so-called *burgalesismo*, a local patriotism of sorts, on whose name a plethora of historical celebrations were organised –mostly paying homage to medieval events and leaders–, and victimised trips to Madrid were arranged, in order to obtain assistance and funds from the central government. On the other end of the social spectrum was the declining group of the craftsmen, who employed untrained labour from the country.

In order to counteract the lay tendencies of the liberal regime, the Burgos Church promoted actions of Catholic militancy, such as the creation of the The Círculo Obrero Burgalés (Burgos Workers Association), founded in 1883 and re-founded in 1902, when a new branch was opened in the southern section of the city, thus increasing the scope of its actions to include assistance, labour and recreational activities.

Politically speaking, the city livened up in 1916, when the populist Zumárraga won the parliamentary elections, which led to the end of the old political system whereby dynastic parties took turns at ruling, and the regional question was brought up, as a way to demand an administrative decentralisation. The dictatorship of Primo de Rivera put an end to these revitalisation attempts.

Demolition of the old Palacio Arzobispal (1914)

From the early 1920's till the outbreak of the Civil War Burgos saw a period of intense economic activity, linked to commerce, to the construction industry, and to the thriving financial activity. The creation of the Sociedad Española de Sedas Artificiales (Spanish Association for Artificial Silks) marked the inception of modern industry in the region. Communications were improved. And there was an intense development of the housing sector: workers' homes were built, with the support of the City Hall and housing coops, leading to the construction of inexpensive, single-family houses with a small garden in different

parts of the city, which marked the direction of the city's future urban expansion. At the same time, a number of buildings were erected in the city centre, inspired in the historicist currents and Modernism, such as the Palacio de Capitanía, the Palacio Episcopal and the Círculo de la Unión, in the Paseo del Espolón, which conferred –and continue to do so today– a special character to the city. The population grew ostensibly, from the 32,000 in 1920 to 40,000 in 1930, and 60,000 in 1940.

A period of hope started with the Second Republic. But the short-lived Bienio Reformista (Reformist Two-Year Period), the tensions during the two years of right-wing ruling, and the military uprising after the triumph of the Frente Popular (Popular Front) truncated all expectations.

Inscription about the Civil War. Palacio de Capitanía General

The coup of July 18, 1936 was supported in Burgos, turning the city into one of the strategic centres of military operations during the Civil War. It was a safe rearguard position, a place of transit or shelter for soldiers, wounded combatants and political prisoners, as well as the venue for diplomatic meetings, ceremonies and military parades. As the capital of the new State, in October of 1937 Franco installed himself in the Palacio de la Isla, where he was to constitute his first government.

During the first half of Franco's ruling (1936-1960), the daily life of the city was immersed in militarism and national-Catholicism, under the power of the Army and the Church, and, like in the rest of Spain, in a struggle for survival. These hungry years would not come to an end until as late as the 1950's. Some companies established their headquarters in the area with the support of the Government, such as the Fábrica Nacional de Moneda y Timbre (Mint) (1953), or through a private initiative, like Cellophane España (1949) or Campofrío, which expanded greatly from 1951 onwards.

Industrial estate of Gamonal-Villimar

In the 1960's Burgos and its province, like many other regions in the country, suffered the greatest rural exodus in history. Several millions of Spaniards emigrated to the industrial centres, mostly Madrid, the Basque Country and Catalonia, as well as to other European countries.

The Polo de Promoción Industrial (Agency for Industrial Promotion), known as Polo de Desarrollo (Development Agency) since 1964, was created in 1964 and soon became instrumental to the deep industrial transformation of the city, turning Burgos into what it is today. The regulations of the time encouraged the creation of industrial estates offering inexpensive land, state subsidies and fiscal exemptions. Both the city's privileged geographical location and the surplus of country labour were taken into consideration. The results were extremely positive.

The population grew rapidly, from 82,000 in 1960 to 120,000 in 1970, 156,000 in 1980, and 162,000 in 1988. The industrial growth reinforced the city's character as a services centre, and the new forms of contemporary life took over traditional culture. The middle classes became larger, the working class consolidated, and the overall living conditions of the population improved substantially.

From then until today, Burgos has advanced along the same road as the rest of the Spanish cities. The social and economic transformations of the 1960's set the conditions for political change, a transition towards democracy that would lead to the establishment of the Spanish Constitution in 1978.

Burgos in the 20th century. Plaza de España

The progress of Burgos is evident today. To see it, just take a stroll around its streets and squares, in the old quarter, or in the new commercial and industrial areas.

Old and new, medieval and modern, the city's current condition is also the result of the following events: a) the creation of a new town around Gamonal when the Polo de Desarrollo was reopened, b) the elimination of the military headquarters of the Calle de Vitoria, which enabled the authorities to expand the old quarter with a new commercial and administrative centre, c) the approval of the Plan General (Delta Sur) and the urban projects north of the river Vena, which physically linked Burgos and Gamonal in the late 1980's and early 1990's, and d) the design of a new Burgos, currently in progress through the Plan del Centro Histórico (Old Quarter Plan) and the revision of the Plan General de Ordenación Urban (General Urban Plan). Not to mention the new single-family housing projects in the periphery and in nearby towns.

The 21st Century

Winter view

At the dawning of the 21st century, the City Hall, as well as the other Public Administrations and the social and economic agents, through the Plan Estratégico de Burgos (Burgos Strategic Plan) (2001-2015), have committed themselves expressly to a series of projects and strategic lines which will play a decisive role in the urban configuration, economic development, cultural promotion and general welfare of the people of Burgos. Expectations are very high. Today Burgos is the only city in Castilla y León with a growing population census. In addition to that, its strategic location, the vigour of its industrial and commercial sectors, and the wealth of its cultural heritage make it a leading city within the region.

Due to its geographic location, at the convergence of three important routes –the one linking the central and northern sections of the peninsu-

la, the one linking Port and Irún, and the Camino de Santiago–, Burgos is destined to become an international meeting point and redistribution centre. Hence the priority given to some infrastructure works, such as the closing of the ring road, the railroad diversion works, or the building of the Burgos airport, next to which will stand a large entrepreneurial and transport centre, featuring a technology park and an inland port with a European projection, capable of organising the transport of goods by land and by sea, through the ports of Bilbao and Santander.

The deep industrial transformation that began in the 1960's still goes on today. Today Burgos is a predominantly industrial city, with a flexible, dynamic entrepreneurial structure, a combination of the entrepreneurial spirit of the local people and the arrival of national and foreign companies. Of particular importance are the automobile parts and the agro-alimentary industries.

Centro Cívico Río Vena

One of the greatest assets of the city is its cultural heritage. The city's long, rich history has left some unique sights and first-class monuments. Visitors can see them first hand or in the pages of this guide-book: the cathedral, the Monasterio de las Huelgas, the Cartuja de Miraflores, the medieval historical complex, the Renaissance town, or the 19th-century bourgeois town, all of them intertwined and overlapped across a city layout dominated by the north-to-south axis of the castle and the river Arlanzón and, east to west, by the Camino de Santiago.

The prehistoric sites of the Sierra de Atapuerca deserve a separate paragraph. Their scientific importance is so great that its social benefits will to a large extent determine the future development of Burgos. The centrally located Solar de la Evolución Humana will house a museum, an auditorium, the Palacio de Exposiciones y Congresos and a research centre, according to the project by Juan Navarro Baldeweg, which intends to be a visual metaphor of the sites of Atapuerca, located by the river Arlanzón, drawing a respectful diagonal line with the cathedral.

The findings of Atapuerca have confirmed the cultural vocation of the city. Burgos breathes culture on a daily basis, a culture that does not hold on to the traditional elements linked to the historical and artistic heritage or to the Spanish language, but manifests itself in multiple avant-garde creations developed –occasionally or in a stable manner– within the framework of the cultural centres or through street performances.

A growing concern for the environment, particularly focused on the parks and gardens along the banks of the river Arlanzón, the development of the local cuisine and the practise of sports are an illustration of the city's extraordinary quality of living.

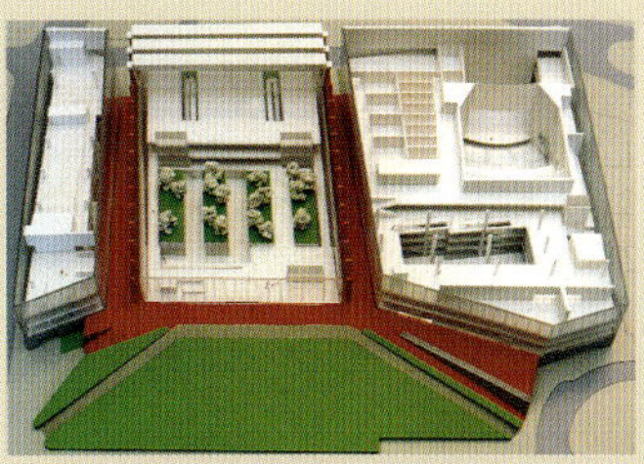

Model, Museo de la Evolución Humana

1 Catedral

The Burgos Cathedral, the city's monumental icon, is, together with the cathedrals of León and Toledo, one of the jewels of Spanish Gothic art.

Catedral

Ground plan of the Burgos Cathedral

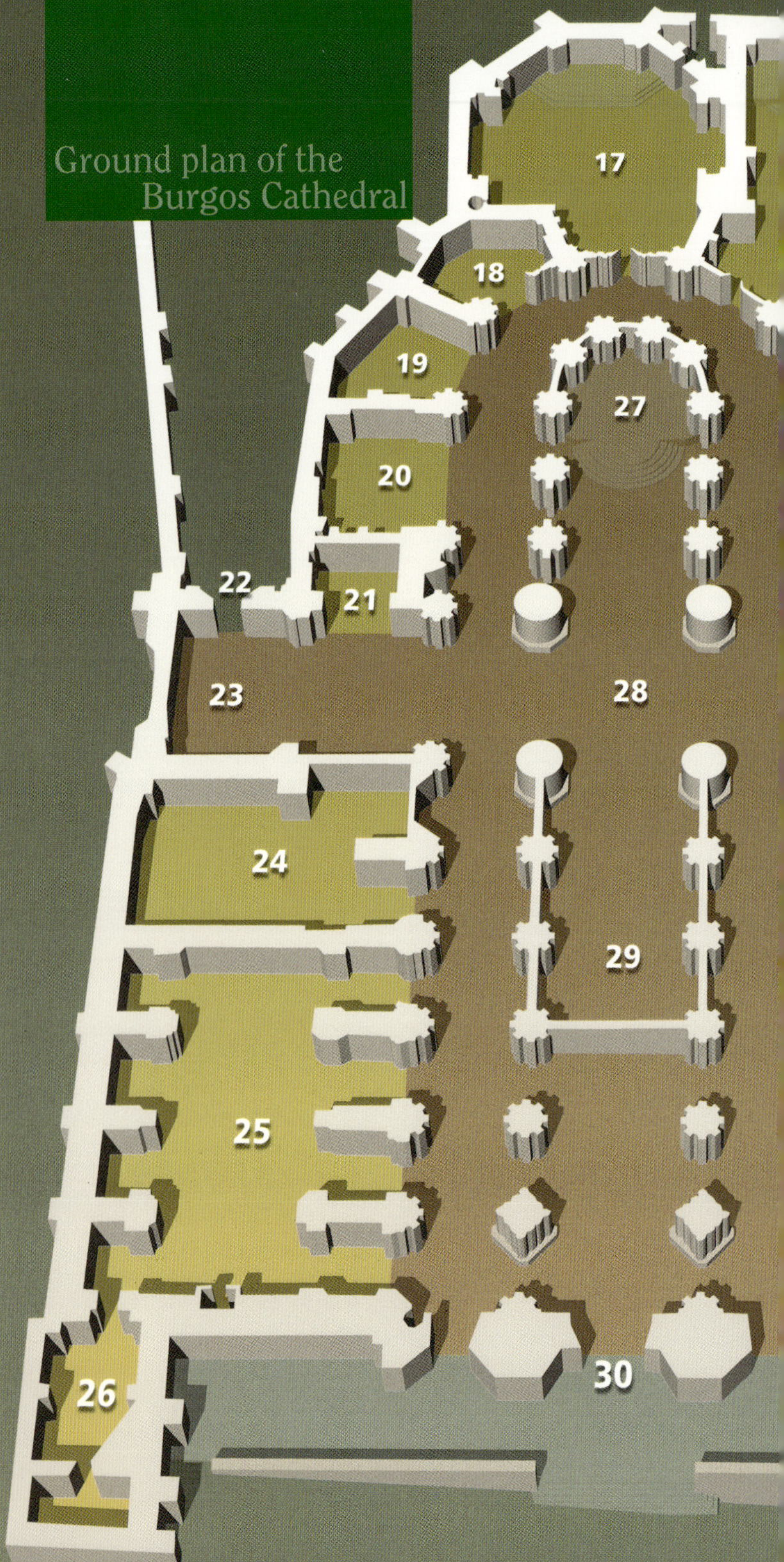

Capilla del Santísimo Cristo de Burgos 1
Chapter Offices 2
Capilla de la Presentación 3
Capilla de las Reliquias 4
Capilla de San Juan de Sahagún 5
Capilla de la Visitación 6
Sala de San Fernando (tourist reception) 7
Cloister 8
Capilla de San Juan Bautista 9
Capilla de Santa Catalina 10
Capilla del Corpus Christi 11
Chapter Room 12
Main Sacristy 13
Ante-sacristy 14
Capilla de San Enrique 15
Capilla de Santiago and Museo 16
Capilla del Condestable 17
Capilla de San Gregorio 18
Capilla de la Anunciación 19
Capilla de la Natividad 20
Capilla de San Nicolás 21
Puerta de la Pellejería 22
Golden Stairway 23
Capilla de la Concepción 24
Capilla de Santa Tecla 25
Sacristy of Capilla de Santa Tecla 26
Main Altar 27
Transept and Dome 28
Choir 29
Puerta de Santa María 30
Puerta del Sarmental 31

We do not know the names of the first masters who took part in the erection of the cathedral, although most likely they were familiar with the French architecture of the time, since the Burgos cathedral bears remarkable similarities with those of Bourges, Chartres, Amiens, Reims, Coutances and Notre Dame in Paris. Master Ricardo, who was involved in the works at the Monasterio de las Huelgas in the early 13th century, might also have been involved in the early stages of the construction of the cathedral, which would account for the similarities between both structures.

Work on the Burgos cathedral began on July 20, 1221, partly on the site of a former Romanesque church erected under Alfonso VI (1065-1109). The king Fernando III and the bishop Mauricio, who during his European trips had become familiar with the new French Gothic style, set the first stone.

The works advanced rapidly and as early as 1230, mass was already being celebrated in the main nave. The altar's end of the church, including the ambulatory and the chancel, was completed in 1257. The naves and the upper and lower cloisters must have been finished in the late 13th century. The eastern chapels of the latter were still being built in the early decades of the 14th century. The first known architect is master Enrique, mentioned in some documents of 1261. It was also Enrique who supervised the construction of the León cathedral. Juan Pérez took over later on; he died in 1296, and his work was continued by a long list of master builders all throughout the 14th century. As a whole, the cathedral was built during the 13th century, but continuous additions, alterations and expansions were made during the following centuries, particularly in the 15th and 16th centuries, coinciding with one of the brightest periods of the city. Although not as important, the 17th and 18th centuries also saw quite a bit of activity.

Capilla del Condestable and dome

However, works on the cathedral virtually came to a halt during the 19th century (with the exception of the marble flooring of the naves). Due mainly to the City Hall's loss of economic power after the sale of the Church lands, the conservation works were neglected, which led to a visible deterioration of the cathedral. The declaration of the cathedral as a National Site in 1887 raised awareness on the need to preserve it. The successful intervention of the architect Vicente Lampérez in the early 20th century saved from ruin so-

me unique elements, such as the spires, and reinforced the building's structure. UNESCO declared the cathedral a World Heritage Site in 1984, which pushed forward the restoration activities. The preservation activities carried out during the last years of the 20th century have greatly improved the condition of the Burgos cathedral.

The cathedral has always been the centre of the city's public life, and some of the key events in the city's history have taken place in or around it. The cathedral was not only the venue for solemn religious celebrations;

During Napoleon's invasion, the French troops raided the cathedral and stole the large late-16th-century metropolitan custody by Juan de Arfe. In 1813, when the French left the city and blew up the castle, the shock wave destroyed most of the Gothic stained-glass windows. The cathedral also witnessed a number of violent events, such as the assassination of the governor Gutiérrez on the Escalera del Sarmental in 1869.

Dome by Juan de Vallejo

important civil events were also held in the cathedral area, in the Plaza del Sarmental and the Plaza de Santa María. The visit to the cathedral was the climatic event during the sojourns of the kings in Burgos. Also, until the Casa del Cordón was erected in the late 15th century, the now gone Palacio Episcopal, attached to the cathedral, served as the temporary residence of the monarchs during their stays in the city. The cathedral was also the stage for transcendental events such as the royal wedding of Luis XIII and Ana of Austria in 1615. But the canonical routine was interrupted not only by these festive events. A number of catastrophes also took place in the cathedral. On March 4, 1539, the old dome collapsed; and in 1642 a violent hurricane blew down most of the spires.

General description

The cathedral has a Latin cross ground plan, with an ambulatory and three naves, the central one being higher and wider than the rest. The transept has a single nave; the dome rests on its convergence with the central nave. The structure is 84 by 54 metres. The Gothic cloister was erected on the south-eastern end in the late 13th century; the old Romanesque cloister was preserved for some time on the south-western side, where, with the passage of time, the Episcopal palaces were built. From the early times of the Gothic temple, a number of apse chapels were erected on the upper end, most of which were either destroyed in subsequent interventions or replaced by new structures. Chapels were also erected, and subsequently destroyed or replaced by new ones, from the 15th century on.

Inside, the structure features the classical arcade/triforium/window Gothic sequence. The building has simple Gothic vaulting, with a longitudinal rib

Right above the royal statues of the main front, around an image of the Virgin, is an inscription of the late 15th century that says: Pulc(h)ra es et Decora, that is, You Are Pure and Beautiful, a clear reference to the Virgin, to whom the cathedral is dedicated. There are two other inscriptions above the bells on both towers. One, next to an image of Saint John the Baptist, says: Ecce Agnus Dei (Here Is the Lamb of God). The other, located on both sides of an image of Cristo Varón de Dolores, says: Pax Vobis (Peace Be With You).

along the central nave. The side chapels feature four-part vaulting. In the area near the dome, damaged by its collapse in 1539, the groined vaults were replaced with curved ribs.

Exterior

The main portal, at the Plaza de Santa María, features three vertical levels. The lower one contains the doors leading into each of the naves of the church. The main door, the Puerta del Perdón, was rebuilt in neo-Classical style by Fernando González de Lara –due to the advanced deterioration of the former Gothic structure. The old set of statues was disposed of. The side doors, originally Gothic also, were reformed in 1663 by the sculptor Juan de Pobes, who made two reliefs with Marian motifs to decorate the tympanums. A golden rose window featuring a David's cross dominates the middle section of

Galería de los Reyes

the main front. The upper level features a gable end containing six mysterious 13-century statues, which might represent monarchs of the Old Testament. On both sides stand the lower sections of each of the towers. On top of the second section of the towers rise the famous **spires**, started in the mid 15th century by Juan de Colonia, at the request of the bishop Alonso de Cartagena, and finished during the episcopate of Luis de

South spire with the anagram of the bishop Cartagena

Acuña in the late 15th century. The spires are topped by small balconies featuring the anagrams JHS, with the escutcheon of Luis de Acuña on the north tower, and SM, related with Alonso de Cartagena, a member of the Santa María family, on the south tower.

As you head towards the Iglesia de San Nicolás, you will reach the Calle de Fernán González, where you will find the **Portada de la Coronería**, also known as Portada de los Apóstoles, located on the northern section of the transept. The jambs feature a sober representation of the apostles –hence the name– and the tympanum contains a large Deesis (scene of the Virgin and Saint John interceding before Christ the Judge). These images are accompanied by angels carrying symbols of the Passion (the cross, the crown of thorns, the nails, the spear and the column). On the lintel stands out a representation of Heaven's gate, containing the scene of the psicostasis, that is, the moment when Saint Michael weighs the souls before allowing them into Heaven. To the right are those who passed the test. All these sculptures were made in the mid 13th century by a Spanish sculptor influenced by French aesthetics. Above the portal and the triple window that lets light into this part of the transept, there is a series of royal figures that might represent members of the Castilian monarchy of the mid 13th century. Further up the Calle de Fernán González you will reach the staircase leading to the Llana de Afuera.

Portada de la Coronería

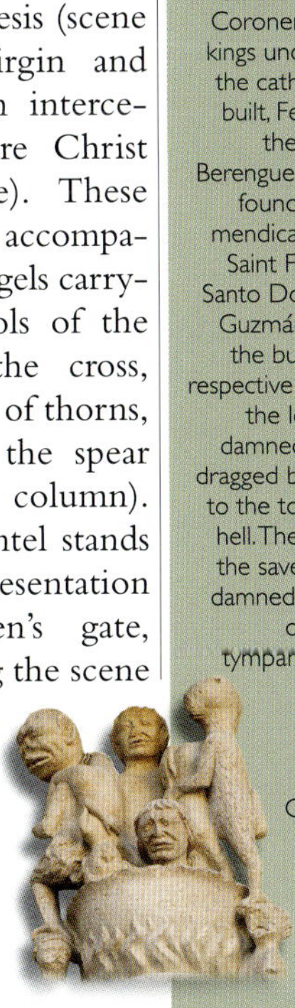

Heaven's Gate. Detail of the Portada de la Coronería

Imploring Virgin, Portada de la Coronería

Among the characters depicted on the Puerta de Coronería are the kings under whom the cathedral was built, Fernando III the Saint and Berenguela, and the founders of the mendicant orders, Saint Francis and Santo Domingo de Guzmán, showing the bulls of their respective orders. To the left are the damned, who are dragged by demons to the torments of hell. The theme of the saved and the damned continues outside the tympanum, in the lower sections of the archivolts. On top are images of angels and cherubs. The furthest archivolt features the resurrection of the dead.

The bas-reliefs in the upper section of the Puerta de la Pellejería are concerned with the martyrdoms of Saint John the Baptist and Saint John the Evangelist. The tympanum features a praying image of the bishop who promoted the works, surrounded by angels, before the image of Saint Mary and, on both sides, the sculptures of Saint Peter and Saint Paul.

Portada de la Pellejería

The **Portada de la Pellejería** was built in 1516, during the episcopate of Juan Rodríguez de Fonseca. It stands on the eastern section of the northern wing of the transept but, unlike the Puerta de la Coronería, it is level with the cathedral floor. It is one of the earliest manifestations of Burgos Renaissance. It was originally designed as an early Plateresque structure by Francisco de Colonia, the last member of this family of artists. There are apostles and saints on the jambs of the arch, following its curvature. On both sides are sculptures of the two Saint Johns, of Santiago (Saint James) and Saint Andrew. The group of sculptures is surrounded by a profusion of Plateresque motifs inspired by Italian models introduced by the Milan artist Antonio de Monza.

There is a wonderful view of the cathedral from the Llana de Afuera. One can see the exterior part of the **Capilla del Condestable**, with its superb sculptures by Simón de Colonia and the coats of arms of the Velasco and Mendoza families. Also noteworthy is the decoration of the sacristy in this chapel, with the repetition of the coat of arms of the Constable. Other family emblems to be found here are the X-shaped cross of Saint Andrew, the Jerusalem cross, and the radiant sun with the JHS anagram, the symbol of Saint Bernardine of Siena, deeply venerated by don Pedro and his wife Mencía and, thanks to whose intercession, tradi-

The coat of arms of Pedro Fernández de Velasco, sustained by two figures, is covered by bell-shaped enamel motifs and trimmed with castles and lions. That of Mencía de Mendoza y Figueroa is divided into different sections and bears the words Ave María (the symbol of the Mendozas) and fig tree leaves (the symbol of the Figueroas).

Capilla del Condestable

tion has it, the Constable's wife became pregnant for the first time.

Along the Calle de Diego Porcelos you will reach the Calle de la Paloma, which surrounds the lower cloister of the cathedral. In the Plaza del Rey San Fernando, at the top of a large stairway, you will reach the **Puerta del Sarmental**. It is the best piece of 13th-century stone sculpture of the cathedral, and one of the best in Spain. The group is completed with figures of the Apostles, located in the lintel, of the Old Men of the Apocalypse, and groups of angels and archangels in the archivolts. The mullion features an image of a bishop, traditionally identified with Mauricio, the founder of the cathedral. This is a replica of the original sculpture, which, due to the risk of deterioration, has been taken inside the cloister. The jambs feature sculptures of Saint Peter and Saint Paul, and of Aaron and Moses; the latter are posterior to the rest of the portal.

Next to the Puerta del Sarmental stands a neo-Gothic structure, on the site of the old **Palacio Episcopal**, which was demolished in 1913. The upper section features two early Gothic arches, part of the previous structure, probably dating from the 12th century.

The Puerta del Sarmental features a beautiful image of the Pantocrator surrounded by the Tetramorfos (a representation of the evangelists in animal form), which accompanies its human depiction. This group of sculpture shows the influence of French models, particularly of the Amiens cathedral.

The bishop Mauricio, Puerta del Sarmental

Puerta del Sarmental

The Papamoscas (Fly Eater) is an interesting mechanic device located on top of the cathedral's clock. It represents a human figure, from the waist up, which every hour on the hour tolls a bell and opens its mouth. Next to it is a smaller figure, the Martinillos, which tolls the bell every quarter of an hour.

The Rosetón del Sarmental is the only Gothic rose window left in the cathedral. Most of the church's original stained glass windows were destroyed in 1813, when the castle was blown up. Around the altar area and in the rose window are some stained glass windows dating from the late 19th century, replacing the original Gothic ones.

INTERIOR

Past the threshold of the main door, in the upper level of the main nave, you will find the friendly figure of the **Papamoscas**. A triforium runs along the whole length of the nave, that is, a gallery on archways, located under the windows, built in the 13th century, although the balustrade was redecorated in the late 15th century, in the time of the bishop Acuña, as indicated by the escutcheons.

From the third level upwards, the main nave is separated from the side naves by the **choir** and a large grille dating from the 17th and 18th centuries. The choir, which originally stood at the altar end of the temple, was moved to the lower end of the main nave in the 16th century. It is closed off by a sober classicist marble structure that began to be built in the area facing the main door in 1604. This structure, known as the retro-choir, was financed by the cardinal Antonio Zapata, whose escutcheons, designed by Juan de Naveda and Felipe de Alvarado, can be seen on the sides. It features a large painting of the early 17th century, attributed to Juan van der Hamenn, representing Saint Anthony the Abbot and Saint Paul the Hermit. They are flanked by two sculptures of Saint Peter and Saint Paul, by the court sculptor Antonio de Riera. The side closings were built in 1659 by Juan de la Sierra, who did his best to harmonise his work with that of Naveda and Alvarado. A series of 1659 canvas paintings by the Benedictine artist Juan Rizi decorate these closing structures. The ones on the right-hand-side nave represent scenes of the Stigmatisation of Saint Francis, the Miracle of the Flowers of Saint Casilda, and the

Retro-choir

Triumph of Saint Julian. The paintings of the left nave represent Saint Anthony of Padua, the Martyrdom of Saint Helen and Saint Centola, and the Martyrdom of Saint Victoria.

Inside the choir, presiding over the whole structure, is the recumbent figure of the founder of the cathedral, the bishop Mauricio. It is a 13th-century sculpture, made of wood and lined with copper, which, originally, was richly decorated with enamels from Limoges and semi-precious stones. The **choir stalls**, arranged in two levels, were carved during the 16th century. Some of the best Burgos sculptors of the time, including Felipe Vigarny, Andrés de Nájera, García Arredondo or Simón de Bueras, participated in this project. Above the stalls are the two large cathedral organs. The Epistle organ was built by Juan de Argüete in 1636, and the Gospel organ by Juan Manuel de Betolaza in 1806. An early 17th-century grille by Juan Bautista Celma separates the choir from the transept.

Choir stalls

The choir stalls feature scenes of the Old and the New Testaments and scenes of the lives of the saints, particularly of those with a stronger connection with Burgos. Of particular interest is the decoration of the episcopal chair, featuring the profane theme of the Kidnapping of Europa. Also beautiful is the woodwork decorating the seats and the backs.

Epistle organ

Fretwork dome interior

When the original dome came down in 1539, the members of the cathedral council and the city hall agreed to build a new dome as soon as possible. The emblem of Burgos was included on the base of the octagonal tambour in order to acknowledge the city hall's collaboration.

In the very centre of the nave, where it converges with the transept, stands the beautiful **dome**, rebuilt by Juan de Vallejo in 1539, although the creator of the project might have been Felipe Vigarny. This impressive octagonal lantern rests on four gigantic pillars. It features the escutcheons of Carlos I, of the city of Burgos –which contributed to its reconstruction–, and of the bishop Álvarez de Toledo. Many sculptures of saints stand on the balconies. On top is the beautiful fretwork dome, with Mudéjar influences. Directly below the dome lies a simple marble tombstone holding the mortal remains of El Cid and his wife Jimena, brought in from the Monasterio de San Pedro de Cardeña in 1921, during the 7th centenary of the cathedral.

The main nave ends at the **presbytery**, built with marble from Carrara in 1864. It contains the tombs, not always accessible, of the Infantes Juan (†1319), Sancho (†1374) and Beatriz (†1381). The **main altarpiece** was carved, starting in 1562, by the brothers Rodrigo and Bartolomé de la Haya. It is a magnificent Romanesque piece, of large proportions, containing relief scenes dealing with the life of the Virgin, sculptures of the Apostles, and the impressive silver sculpture of Saint Mary Major, to whom the ca-

Dome pillars

The main altarpiece of the cathedral is one of the greatest pieces of its class in Spain. Romanesque in style, it bears the influence of the great Italian Mannerist sculptures. The purpose of all the images is to exalt the figure of the Virgin, to whom the cathedral is dedicated, with scenes and characters connected with her life.

thedral is dedicated, dating from the late 15th century. The images of the Assumption and the Coronation located above the sculpture of the matron saint are by the great sculptor Juan de Anchieta. The painters Diego de Urbina and Gregorio Martínez gilded the piece. The large tabernacle of the altarpiece's bench is by Domingo de Bérriz. In compliance with the decrees of the Council of Trent, relative to the cult of relics, the designers of the altarpiece placed in the lower section of the altarpiece the mortal remains of the saints Elena and Centola, and saint Victoria, brought in from Siero (Burgos) and Cologne, respectively, in 1320, and deeply venerated in the Burgos dioceses.

The first **chapel** of the Epistle nave, that is, the nave on the right, is the **Capilla del Santo Cristo de Burgos**. Although heavily altered in the early 20th century, it conserves an evident primitive look. It corresponds with one of the old walls of the cloister of the Romanesque cathedral, since it was erected on top of it. Its main feature is the neo-Gothic altarpiece, containing the sculptu-

The image of Santa María la Mayor, presiding over the altarpiece, was donated to the cathedral by the bishop Luis de Acuña in the late 15th century.

Holy Christ of Burgos

Legend has it that it was sculpted by Nicodemus and worshipped by the early Christians in Jerusalem and Syria, until, lest it fell in heathen hands, they put it in a box and threw it into the sea, in the hope it would reach a place where it would also be worshipped. And that is exactly what happened: a Burgos merchant found it floating in the water, picked it up, brought it to Burgos and gave it to the Augustine order. It soon became famous due the miracles that were attributed to it.

re of the Holy Christ of Burgos. This sculpture, dating probably from the 14th century, was brought to the cathedral from the Convento de San Agustín in 1860. It is a wooden image, covered with tanned animal hide, to which fake hair has been added, and has always been considered a miraculous piece. The chapel contains a large number of tombs, some of them dating from the 13th century, and others from the 19th.

Juan de Matienzo started work on the **Capilla de la Consolación**, also known as **Capilla de San José**, in 1519, at the request of the canon Gonzalo Diaz de Lerma. It is covered by a large, carved, octagonal star vault.

Capilla de la Consolación

Mortuary portrait of Gonzalo Díaz de Lerma

In the centre of the chapel lies the tomb of the founder, carved around 1524 by Felipe Vigarny. Particularly noteworthy is the beautiful arcosolium, attached to the temple's pillar, where the canon Jacobo de Bilbao lies buried.

Next is the **Capilla de San Juan de Sahagún**, formerly known as the Capilla de los Rojas. It contains a 1765 Rococo altarpiece by José Cortés, with a magnificent sculpture of the patron saint by the Madrid court artist Juan Pascual de Mena. This chapel leads to the **Capilla de las Reliquias**, a late Baroque structure designed by the Carmelite architect José de San Juan de la Cruz and erected by Fernando González de Lara in 1761. The altarpieces in this chapel contain the rich and interesting relic collection of the cathedral.

On the south transept-arm there is a beautiful **rose window** decorated with the only stained glass from the 14th century that survived the explosion of 1813, and accompanied by other stained glass windows dating from the 19th century. The south transept-arm opens into the

The Neoclassic altarpiece of the Capilla de San José is presided by a canvas painting of the Holy Family by Sebastiano del Piombo, brought from Rome by Don Gonzalo: it is one of the best early-16th-century Italian paintings in Spain.

Capilla de la Visitación

In the centre of the Capilla de la Visitación is the beautiful sepulchre of the bishop, maybe built by the workshop of Juan de Colonia. Next to it are other arcosolium sepulchres of, among others, Alfonso Rodríguez de Maluenda, García Ruiz de la Mota, the Calahorra bishop Juan Díez de Coca and the Burgos canon Luis Garcés de Maluenda, all of them dating from the late 15th and the early 16th centuries.

Capilla de la Visitación, containing the tomb of the bishop Alonso de Cartagena, who had a spacious burying space built for himself, his family and his servants. The structure was designed by Juan de Colonia in 1445. The main altarpiece dates from the 17th century, and features paintings influenced by Italian models.

Sepulchre of Alonso de Cartagena

The jambs of the cloister's door were probably made by Gil de Siloe in the late 15th century, and feature scenes representing Jesus entering Jerusalem and the Descent into Limbo, next to the seating figures of Saint Peter and Saint Paul.

Sepulchre of the archbishop Peralta

The furniture of the sacristy includes three altarpieces, dominating the room, and the chests of drawers, all of them Rococo. Both the drawers and the altarpieces are decorated with a series of earlier paintings, dating from around 1700, by a painter connected to the Italian master Luca Giordano.

Opposite this chapel stands the **cloister's doorway**, built in the late 13th century. Its jambs feature a set of sculptures representing the Annunciation, the king David, and the prophet Isaiah. It is one of the few stone works keeping the traces of the original polychrome job. In the tympanum there is a representation of the Baptism of Christ.

Capilla de San Enrique

The **Capilla de San Enrique** was built during the first years of the second half of the 17th century, by fusing two old chapels together. It was erected by Bernabé de Hazas and Juan de la Sierra in the early Baroque style, at the request of the bishop Enrique de Peralta y Cárdenas, whose bronze praying statue stands in an cove near the main altarpiece, probably built by Policarpo de la Nestosa in 1665. The 15th-century statue of the Ecce Homo is a magnificent Flemish work from the Antwerp school. This image is flanked by the statues of two archangels and, on top, the image of Saint Henry. Also noteworthy are the wooden statues of Saint Andrew and the Magdalene, made in the workshop of Gil de Siloe, which stand in a Baroque side altarpiece, and the magnificent chapel organ. Past this chapel you will reach the ambulatory.

Main sacristy

The **ante-sacristy** is presided by the typical brazier, an 18th-century work at the service of the main altarpiece. The **sacristy**, topped by an ample oval dome, was built thanks to the economic legacy of the archbishop Juan Francisco Guillén. It was designed by

Brazier, sacristy

the Carmelite architect José de San Juan de la Cruz. Of particular interest is the exultant Rococo decoration of Marian scenes in the vault.

The **Capilla de Santiago** stands on the site of an old chapel pulled down in 1521. It was designed by Juan de Vallejo. It is an ample space covered by star vaults and dominated by a 1772 late Baroque altarpiece by Fernando González de Lara, dedicated to the patron saint of Spain. At the entrance lies the singular sepulchre of Juan Ortega de Velasco, the abbot of San Quirce, who is represented lying down, flanked by anthropomorphic pilasters, probably the work of Juan de Vallejo. Other interesting tombs are those of the Astudillo-Paredes family, dating from around 1542. This chapel is linked to the Capilla de San Juan, which leads to the cloister: they are home to the Museo Catedralicio.

Sepulchre of the abbot of San Quirce

Main altarpiece, Capilla de Santiago

In the **ambulatory**, the rear side of the altar is decorated with five large relief panels representing the cycle of the Passion. They are all included in a rich late Gothic structure, built, among others, by Simón de Colonia. The first panel, representing the Prayer at the Orchard, and the last one, representing the Ascension, were carved between 1681 and 1683 by Pedro Alonso de los Ríos, a Valladolid sculptor, in a rich Baroque style. Much more interesting are the three central scenes. The first one, showing the Way to Calvary, is a dynamic 1498 composition by Felipe Vigarny (this is his first documented work in Burgos). One of doorjambs of the city of Jerusalem features the earliest *a candelieri* Renaissance decoration in Burgos. The City Hall was so pleased with this work that the artist was immediately commissioned to carry out the next two works: the Crucifixion and the Descent and Burial of Christ, which were completed in 1500 and 1503. Unfortunately, these two works have been damaged by the so-called "stone illness".

The Way to Calvary

Crucifixion

Descent and burial of Christ

The three bas-reliefs of the cathedral's ambulatory, by Felipe Vigarny, mark the beginning of Renaissance sculpture in Burgos.

The **Capilla de la Purificación**, also known as **Capilla del Condestable**, stands on the site of an old chapel dedicated to Saint Peter, at the altar end of the cathedral. Past the door, richly decorated with sculptures by members of the workshop of Simón de Colonia and closed off by a large 1523 grille by Cristóbal de Andino, you will see the only remnants of the old chapel: the tombs of the bishops Rodrigo de Quexada (†1313) and Domingo de Arroyuelo (†1380), located on both sides of the door. This chapel is, without a doubt, one of the most significant late 15th-century structures in the kingdom of Castile. In order to build it, they had to demolish not only the old Capilla de San Pedro, but also a number of houses that at the time were attached to the cathedral in the La Llana area. It was erected thanks to the patronage of the powerful Constable Pedro Fernández de Velasco and his wife Mencía de Mendoza, daughter of the Marquis of Santillana. The great Simón de Colonia began this work in 1482 and finished it, from the structure point of view, in 1494. His son Francisco made the Plateresque access door to the sacristy. The chapel has a central ground plan, as it is habitual with most funereal chapels, although it features a number of irregulari-

The sepulchre of the founders must have been built by Vigarny around 1525, although some experts say it is the work of the Italian sculptor Juan de Lugano. It is an idealised marble depiction of the founders, many years after their death. Next to this funereal structure stands a large red jasper block, which was meant to support the recumbent figure of Pedro and Mencías' grandson, but it was never completed.

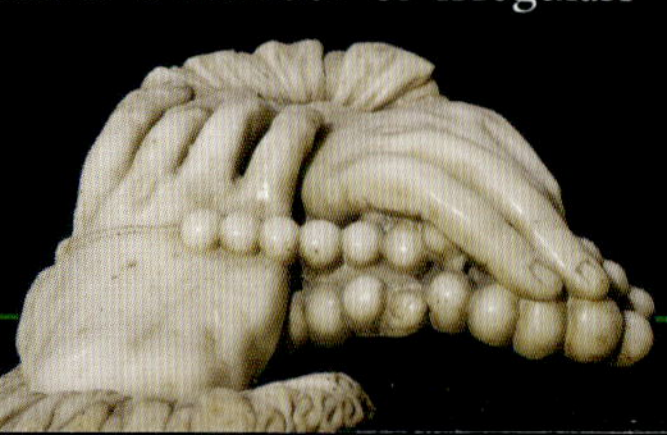

ties, due to the existing conditions prior to its construction. It is topped by an octagonal fretted vault illustrating the impressive building skills of the architect. The chapel is dedicated to the Purification. Light pours in through the gigantic windows featuring stained glass figures by the Flemish artist Arnao de Flandes, dating from the early 16th century. Of particular interest is the triforium that runs along the walls and the impressive coats of arms of the Velasco and Mendoza families, leaning towards the altarpiece and supported, in the upper part, by figures representing wild men and women.

Particularly noteworthy is the main sculpture group, which was made by both artists together. The delicate figures of the Virgin, the Child Jesus, Saint Joseph and the female servant are by Siloe, as well as the more severe ones of old Simeon and the prophetess Ana de Vigarny. Both sculptors also worked together on the base scenes and the top figures.

Altarpiece of Saint Peter

Behind the altar stands the impressive altarpiece representing the Purification. It is a Renaissance work that might have been designed by Vigarny. Diego de Siloe had a decisive role in its construction. He, in fruitful competition with León Picardo and Vigarny, also participated in the gilding and painting of the work, which was carved between 1523 and 1526. The late Gothic altarpiece of Saint Anne is by Gil de Siloe, who carved it in 1500; when he died, the unfinished work was completed by his son, Diego. The 1523 altarpiece of Saint Peter is also the work of Siloe and Vigarny. The most interesting piece is the beautiful statue of Saint Jerome Penitent, influenced by Siloe. The stalls are also by Vigarny, who finished them in 1528.

Figure of Saint Jerome, Retablo de San Pedro

Altarpiece of Saint Anne

Of particular interest among the paintings is the image of the Magdalene, by Gian Pietro Ricci, a disciple of Leonardo da Vinci.

The **Capilla de San Gregorio** maintains its original 13th-century structure, although its access area was altered in the 16th century. It contains the tombs of Gonzalo de Hinojosa (†1327) and Lope de Fontecha (†1351). **The Capilla de la Anunciación**, also known as Capilla de San Antón, is the first one on the Gospel nave, as it converges with the ambulatory. It was erected in the 13th century. Its main feature is the 1540 Renaissance altarpiece by Juan de Lizarazu. The **Capilla de la Natividad** stands on the site of two old Gothic chapels. In 1557, Ana de Espinosa, the widow of Pedro González Salamanca, decided to use the money that her relatives had sent her from Peru to have a funereal chapel built in the cathedral. The project was approved by the City Council, and the works began in 1562, under the supervision of Martín de Bérriz, who built a Mannerist space covered with an oval vault. The altarpiece was built by Martín de la Haya and Domingo de Bérriz in the late 16th century, in a clearly Romanist style. Of particular interest are the stalls, made at the same time as the altarpiece, also by Martín de la Haya.

Sepulchre of the archdeacon Fernando de Villegas

Behind the Capilla de la Natividad is the early 16th-century **sepulchre of Pedro Fernández de Villegas**, attributed to Simón de Colonia.

On the north transept-arm is the **Capilla de San Nicolás**, one of the oldest and most singular spaces in the cathedral. It is known to have been under construction as early as 1230. The vault ribs rest on corbels, an indication of the influence of the Cistercian architectural workshops of the Monasterio de las Huelgas. Sobriety and smoothness are its main characteristics.

But, without a doubt, the most interesting piece in this part of the cathedral is the

Today, the Capilla de San Nicolás holds the early-13th-century sarcophaguses, which used to be in the Capilla de San Enrique, and the restored pre-Gothic altarpiece of Mave (Palencia).

Capilla de San Nicolás

Golden Stairway

superb **Escalera Dorada** (Golden Stairway), designed in 1519 by Diego de Siloe, who at the time had just arrived from Italy, at the request of the archbishop Juan Rodríguez de Fonseca. It is a smart architectural solution, since, in a minimum space, and without blocking the access to the Puerta de Pellejería, it allows to climb the slope between the Puerta de la Coronería and the cathedral floor. It has a straight upwards stretch, which then splits into two diverging side flights converging on the upper door. When making it, the young Siloe must have had in mind some of the great Roman architectural projects, such as the ones designed by Bramante for the staircase of the Cortile Belvedere in the Vatican. Siloe used a profuse decoration of fantastic figures, drawing inspiration from Italian engravers such as Nicoleto Rosex da Modena, Agostino de Musi, Antonio de Monza and Giovanni da Brescia. Also, some of the reliefs representing human figures show the influence of the famous nudes painted by Michelangelo in the Sistine Chapel, which Siloe must have seen shortly after their completion. The golden iron balustrade (which gave the name to the stairway) was forged by the French artist Hilario in 1522.

Next to the Golden Stairway and opposite the Capilla de San Nicolás is a large canvas painting, donated to the cathedral by the archbishop Navarrete, a work by Nicolás de la Cuadra dating from 1718 and representing a miracle of San Juan de Ortega, a well known 11-century Burgos saint, who promoted the Jacobean pilgrimage by improving the hospital network in the Montes de Oca

Back in the Gospel nave, at the lower end of the temple, you will find the **Capilla de la Concepción**, also known as **Capilla de Santa Ana**, which opens into the temple by means of two large arches with two wrought-iron gates built by Luis de Paredes in the late 15th century. In 1477, the bishop Luis de Acuña y Osorio asked the City Council for permission to build a funereal chapel. Once the building licence was granted, he combined two small chapels, the Capilla de Santa Ana and the Capilla de San Antolín. Juan and Simón de Colonia took part in the building process, which finished in 1483. The rectangular space is covered by an impressive vault decorated with engrailed motifs typical of the Colonia family.

The main altarpiece was built by Gil de Siloe between 1486 and 1492, and Diego de la Cruz did the polychrome job, which was subsequently covered by an unfortunate painting intervention in 1868. A recent restoration brought out the original colours and the interesting mural paintings representing the Two Thieves. The altarpiece, similar to a tapestry, deals with the Mystery of the Conception of Mary. On the bench, flanked by a scene of the Resurrection, you will find the figures of Saint Peter and Saint Paul, and of the Four Evangelists.

At the centre of the altarpiece is a large sculpture group representing the apocryphal passage of the Embrace of Saint Joachim and Saint Anne before Jerusalem's Golden Gate, when, tradition has it, Saint Anne became miraculously pregnant with the Virgin Mary.

Main altarpiece

The bishop Acuña, main altarpiece

On top is the patriarch Jetse, lying down and asleep. Out of his chest grows a two-branch tree representing the kings of Judeah, the ancestry of Jesus Christ. The branches come together in the top, by means of a seated Virgin and Child flanked by the figures of the Church and the Synagogue. On the sides there is a series of relief scenes, such as the figure of the chapel's patron saint, the bishop Acuña, who is represented praying, surrounded by clergymen, among whom is his assistant Fuentepelayo, holding a devotional book. Opposite this is the scene describing the miracle of the holy hunter Saint Hubert. The upper reliefs complete the apocryphal story of the conception and birth of Mary. The narration starts, in the top left relief, with the expulsion of Joachim and Anne from the temple due to the stigma of her sterility. On the right-hand side is the apparition of the angel to Joachim, announcing his paternity. Back to the left, there is a relief showing the birth of Mary and, to the right, the Presentation of Mary in the Temple. At the top of the altarpiece, above the Episcopal symbols of Acuña, are the dramatic figures of Calvary, set against the already mentioned background paintings of the Good and Bad Thieves.

To the left of the entrance to this chapel is the great sepulchre of the archdeacon Fernando Díaz de Fuentepelayo, a loyal defender of Acuña. It was probably made by members of the workshop of Simón de Colonia, with the possible collaboration of the workshop of Gil de Siloe.

There is yet another important work in this chapel, a small stone altarpiece built by Diego de Siloe and his workshop in 1522, dedicated to Saint Anne. It features a very interesting painting of the Holy Family and San Juanito, attributed to the great 16th-century Italian painter Andrea del Sarto.

The founder's sepulchre was not built during his lifetime, but in 1519. Diego de Siloe achieved an extremely delicate work, showing his knowledge of the flat bas-reliefs of Donatello and the structure of the sepulchre of the pope Sixtus IV by Pollaiolo.

The **Capilla de Santa Tecla** stands at the lower end of the temple, and opens into the Gospel nave by means of four arches reminiscent of the four 14th-century chapels that were combined in order to built this great Baroque structure. Work on this chapel stared in 1731, promoted by the archbishop Manuel de Samaniego y Jaca, who had previously governed the dioceses of Tarragona, whose matron saint is Santa Tecla. By building this chapel, he intended to introduce in Burgos the devotion to this saint. The project, whose designer remains unknown, was supervised by Andrés Collado. Other architects and artists, such as Francisco Baztigueta and Narciso Cortés, participated in the project. The structure of the chapel orbits around a space with a large half-sphere lowered cupola and two intermediate rib vaults that give an indication of what the original vaulting may have looked like. The space is richly decorated with painted plaster pieces by Juan de Areche, who created images of evangelists and saints, surrounded by a profusion of vegetal motifs.

This chapel features an outstanding main altarpiece. Its author is unknown, although he must have been a member of the circle of Cortés del Valle and José Valdán, very active in Burgos in the mid 18th century. On top of a large base stands the main section, divided into three vertical parts by means of four stipitis. The central section features the martyrdom of Santa Tecla, anachronistically including Moorish executioners instead of Roman ones, made by an member of the group of the Íscar sculptor Alejandro Carnicero.

Image of the martyrdom of Santa Tecla

The upper section of the altarpiece of the Capilla de Santa Tecla features three small sculptures of the Child Jesus, Saint Ignatius and Saint Francis Xavier. The side sections feature San Antón and Santo Domingo de la Calzada. The piece is topped by a lively sculpture of Santiago Matamoros (Saint James the Moorslayer).

The **upper cloister** may be reached via the ante-sacristy or through the south transept-arm. The cloister was built in the late 13th and early 14th centuries. The angles feature four interesting sculpture groups representing scenes of the childhood of Christ and members of the Castilian royalty. On the corridor walls are sculptures of Alfonso X and Violante, plus different biblical characters. Next to them is a remarkable series of 15th- and 16-century tombs, mostly of cathedral clergymen, such as the one of the canon Santander, by Diego de Siloe. Also outstanding is the so-called Sepulcro de Mudarra, a Romanesque sculpture from the Monasterio de San Pedro de Arlanza.

Upper cloister

Sepulchre of the canon Santander

On the eastern side of the cathedral, the first chapel you will see is the **Capilla de San Juan Bautista**. Although erected by the bishop Juan Cabeza de Vaca in the early 15th century, today's structure dates from the 16th century. The chapel is linked to the Capilla de Santiago (described above), and both house the **Museo Catedralicio**. This museum, designed according to modern exhibition criteria, con-

One of the most impressive sculptures in the museum is that of Christ being whipped, by Diego de Siloe.

The collection of paintings includes an interesting series of works by old Flemish and Spanish-Flemish artists, such as brother Alonso de Zamora. There are also some pre-Renaissance board paintings from the early 16th century, by Alonso de Sedano and the Maestro de los Balbases, which is all that is left of the old relic altarpiece. Of particular interest are the board painting representing Pentecost's by Pedro de Campaña and some canvases from the late 16th century, such as the Annunciation by Gregorio Martínez.

Museo Catedralicio

tains a rich collection of sculptures, paintings and silverwork. There is also an interesting collection of Baroque canvases, including works by the great Burgos painter Mateo Cerezo the Young, such as his magnificent Christ in Agony. Among the most interesting pieces of silverware are the metropolitan cross, by Juan de Arfe, the reliquaries of Saint Peter, Saint Paul and Saint James (Santiago), attributed to Juan González de Frías and donated by the bishop Acuña in the late 15th century, and the pieces of the altar of the Capilla del Condestable, such as the late 15th-century chalice and the Burgundy *portapaz*.

The next chapel opening into the cloister is the **Capilla de Santa Catalina**. It is accessed via an interesting 14th-century portal, with a tympanum showing the scene of the Descent of the

Metropolitan cross

Cáliz del Condestable

Capilla de Santa Catalina

Cross. It is an impressive quadrangular space topped by a large star vault. It was built in the mid 14th century, and was once used as the Chapter Room and, occasionally, as the meeting place of the Burgos City Hall during the Middle Ages and, more recently, as sacristy. The drawers were designed by Pedro Martínez. On the walls hang the portraits of all the bishops and archbishops of the Burgos dioceses.

Capilla del Corpus Christi

The **Capilla del Corpus Christi** leads to the cloister through a 14th-century portal whose tympanum contains a Deesis and, below it, the praying figures of Juan Estébanez, the founder of the chapel, and his wife. It is a somewhat irregular space, of little architectural interest, containing the so-called **Cofre del Cid** (10)*, the chest which, tradition has it, the Castilian hero handed to the Jews Rachel and Vidas, although, in reality, it is probably an old chest used to keep the documents of the Council.

Mudejar coffered ceiling, Chapter Room

From this chapel, a stairway leads to the **Chapter Archives and Library**. Below it, two niches contain the recumbent figures of the counts of Castañeda, brought in from the Convento de la Trinidad, which follow the model employed in the sepulchral effigies of the constables. This chapel leads to the 15th-century **Chapter Room** (reformed in the 16th century), which features an interesting Mudéjar artesonado ceiling with *mocárabes*. Today, it holds interesting Flemish and Hispano-Flemish paintings.

Virgin and Child. Anonymous Flemish artist

The last chapel, the **Capilla de San Jerónimo**, stands on the north-west end of the cloister. It is a small quadrangular space with a fretted cross vault, and was built in the mid 16th century. It has an altarpiece attributed to Diego Guillén.

Detail of the Adoration of the Magi. Diego de la Cruz

* *This and the other numbers in parenthesis refer to the chapter or route where the quoted object or building are described.*

2 Around the Catedral

Around the cathedral are interesting samples of the different historical stages the city has gone through. Particularly noteworthy are the medieval town, the Renaissance city and the city of the Enlightment.

Around the Catedral

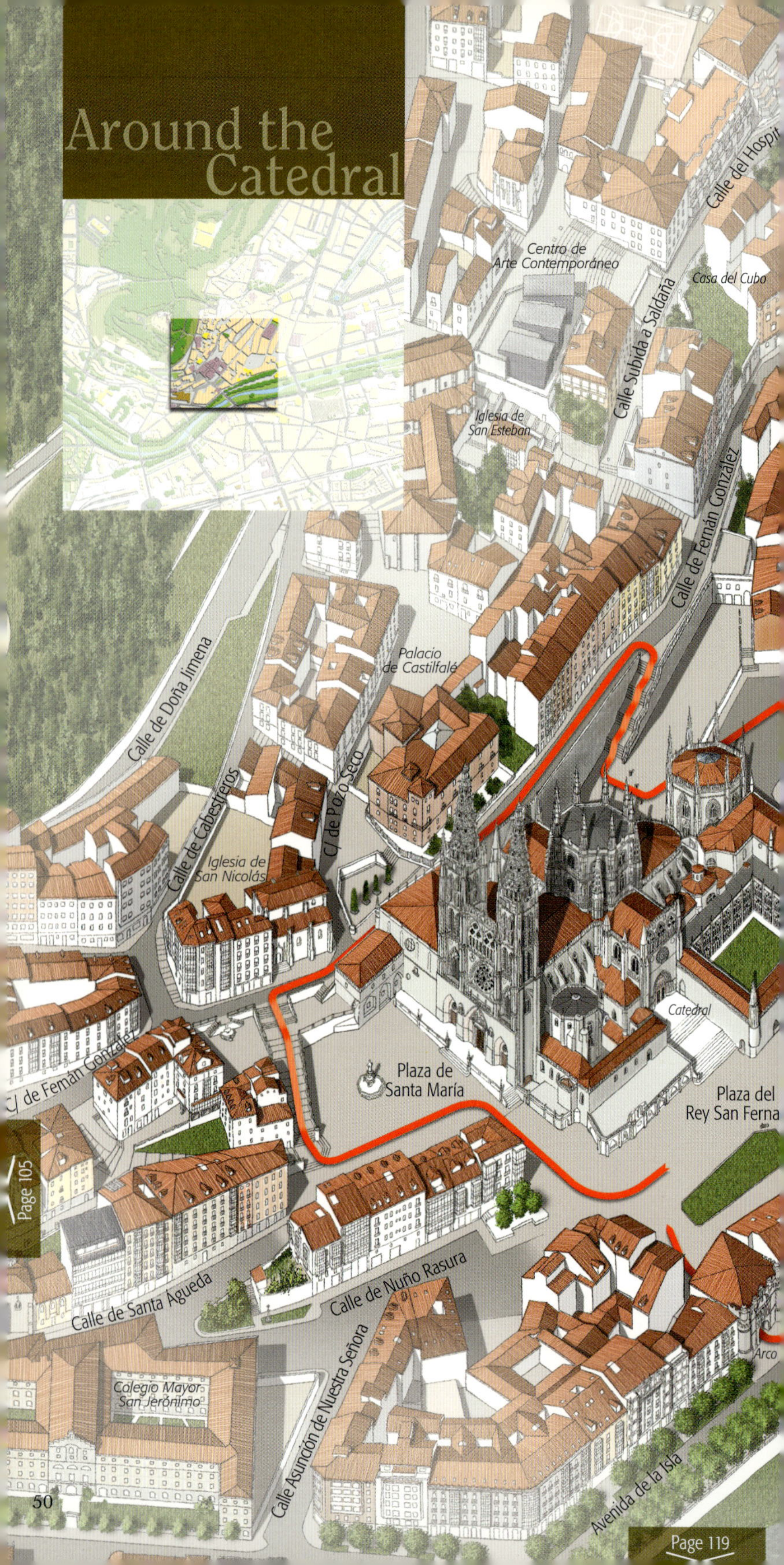

Page 105

Page 119

Calle de Fernán González
C/ de San Gil
Arco del Pilar
Iglesia de San Lorenzo
C/ de Fernando III El Santo
Plaza del Huerto del Rey
Calle de Laín Calvo
Calle de San Carlos
Calle de San Lorenzo
Calle del Almirante Bonifaz
Calle del Cardenal Segura
C/ de la Virgen de la Paloma
Calle de Diego Porcelos
C/ de la Sombrerería
Plaza Mayor
Estatua de Carlos III
Ayuntamiento
Consulado del Mar
Paseo del Espolón
Río Arlanzón
Puente de Santa María
Calle de Valladolid
Plaza de Vega

Page 106

A short walk around the cathedral will give you a more accurate idea of the different stages that the city by the Arlanzón has gone through over the years: the Gothic city (13th-15th centuries), the Renaissance city (16th century) and the bourgeois city (18th and 19th centuries). On the façades of the towers, as you walk clockwise, you will see the following:

PLAZA DE SANTA MARÍA

It has stood at the foot of the cathedral since the 15th century, when the convert bishop Pablo de Santamaría ordered the demolition of all the houses and marketplaces that were attached to the walls of the cathedral. Today's structure dates from the 17th century, when the fountain with the images of the Virgin and Child with cherubs was built at the request of Clemente de Quintana.

Plaza de Santa María

Virgin and Child, Plaza de Santa María

Further up, in the direction of the Iglesia de San Nicolás, is the old **Calle del Azogue** (market), one of the main trading points of the medieval city. The houses where Fadrique Alemán de Basilea, Juan de la Junta and Martín de Guía installed the city's first press in the late 15th century have been preserved. In that press were printed some famous works, such as the first edition of *La Celestina* (1499), *Lazarillo de Tor-*

mes, the *Biblia de Maguncia* or *Las antigüedades de España*, by Antonio de Nebrija.

The **Iglesia de San Nicolás** stands on a previous Romanesque structure. Its erection began in the early 14th century, with a donation of the bishop Juan Cabeza de Vaca, and continued throughout the following century thanks to different contributions.

Inside the sober structure, the south front stands out; it faces the cathedral and has a pointed arch, archivolts with figures and vegetal motifs, an ogee arch and a tympanum featuring the seated statue of Saint Nicholas lecturing, accompanied by Saint Sebastian and Saint Vitores, a local saint, holding his head in his hand.

Main front, Iglesia de San Nicolás

The church has three three-section naves, with ribbed vaulting and a choir with a richly decorated cover, probably by Simón de Colonia. Of particular interest is the monumental main altarpiece, made of stone and dating from the early 16th century (1504). The merchant Gonzalo López Polanco commissioned its construction to Simón de Colonia, who was assisted by his son Francisco de Colonia.

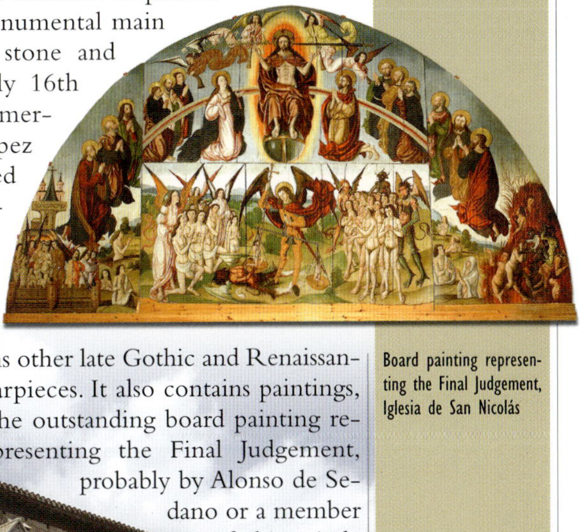

Board painting representing the Final Judgement, Iglesia de San Nicolás

The church contains other late Gothic and Renaissance tombs and altarpieces. It also contains paintings, such as the outstanding board painting representing the Final Judgement, probably by Alonso de Sedano or a member of his circle (circa 1515).

Ascent towards San Nicolás from Plaza de Santa María

The altarpiece is rather a sepulchre-altarpiece, due to the tombs located on both sides of its lower section, belonging to the benefactor and his relatives. It is a Gothic structure, with some Renaissance elements in the sculptures.

Main altarpiece, Iglesia de San Nicolás

Access to the church is via the **Calle de Fernán González**, a long street agglutinating the former Calles de San Llorente, Coronería, Tenebregosa and Viejarrúa, where all the craft activities once concentrated, as well as the commerce, the religious edifices, the Camino de Santiago and, in general, the daily life of the city, for locals and strangers alike, until modern times. Further east along this street, past the Palacio de Castilfalé (7), to the left, and the cathedral's Puerta de la Coronería (1), to the right, you will

Houses along Calle Fernán González

descend a large stairway next to the altar end of the cathedral in order to reach Las Llanas.

Arch communicating the two Llanas

■ Llana de Afuera and Llana de Adentro

Since the 13th century, these spaces were used for the exhibition and sale of the cereal products, mainly bread, consumed in the city. Activity concentrated in the area between the Puerta de Santa María, the entrance point for the products, and Las Llanas. The products were weighed and measured under the strict vigilance of the delegates of the abbess of the Monasterio de las Huelgas, the matron saint of Las Llanas, who, thanks to a privilege granted by Alfonso VIII, had the right to collect a tax consisting of a small amount of wheat on the value of the product that had not been sold. There were many lawsuits and complaints on the part of the neighbours, the council and the monastery, due to abusive practices in the tax co-

Llana de Afuera

Palacio de Castilfalé

Llana de Adentro

llection process and to disagreements between different jurisdictions.

Past the Llana de Afuera, along the Calle del Cardenal Segura, amidst houses, galleries and restaurants adapted to the layout of the old medieval town, you will reach the Plaza Mayor.

Plaza Mayor and Casa Consistorial

Both buildings were erected in the 18th century, but their origins go further back in time. Since the late Middle Ages, the square had held the city's Small Market, where staple products were sold and popular celebrations took place.

The Casa Consistorial was built on the site of the old Puerta de las Carretas, a minor wall gate located betwe-

Plaza Mayor

en the Puerta de San Pablo and the Puerta de Santa María, which led directly to the marketplace. On top of this gate, as early as the 16th century, the members of the Regimiento, who needed their own space to show their power and prestige, until then restricted to the upper floor of the Puerta de Santa María and overshadowed by the nearby cathedral and the Episcopal palace, set up a presidential tribune of sorts, from which they could enjoy the celebrations (bullfighting, fireworks, weddings of illustrious people, etc.). The most radical transformations, however, took place during the Enlightenment, well into the 18th century. The building of a new classicist City Hall began in 1784, designed

Casa Consistorial (City Hall)

by the Burgos architect Fernando González de Lara and subsequently modified by Ventura Rodríguez. Its inauguration in 1791 was to have deep consequences on the life of the city.

The building of the City Hall caused the demolition of the Puerta de las Carretas and the adjacent wall, and the green light was given to build new lined-up edifices, with arcades around the square. On the north side, the old trading space became the Plaza Mayor. In the meantime, on the south side, outside the wall and next to the river, alongside of the road connecting France and Madrid, a new and modern horizon opened up, turning its back on the old city and embellished with a landscaped garden.

Paseo del Espolón

The biggest people-watching venue in the modern city. As indicated above, the construction of the new Casa Consistorial on the site of the former Puerta de las Carretas led to the demolition of the wall and to the design of a series of gardens on the banks of the river Arlanzón, in the old Ronda del Espolón, between the Puerta de San Pablo and the Puerta de Santa María.

The isolated, closed-in Burgos of the past gave way to a new city that pulled down the wall and looked outwards, towards progress, with a line of buildings running parallel to the river. The river Arlanzón lost its traditional role as a defensive moat and became the centre of the city's layout, perfectly channelled by a splendid stone wall. The Espolón became the centre of the 19th-century city, a space to see and be seen, designed by the leading bourgeoisie to meet its needs and aesthetic tastes.

In 1784, at the request of the prior of the Consulado del Mar and mayor of the city, Antonio Tomé, an illustrated man and a wealthy wool trader, a statue of Carlos III was erected in the middle of the square, designed by the Murcia sculptor Alfonso and sculpted by Domingo de Urquiza, in acknowledgement to the assistance the monarch had given to the city.

Paseo del Espolón

The Academia de Dibujo was erected by Manuel Eraso at the initiative of the Consulado del Mar in the late 18th century.

Paseo del Espolón

Statue of Enrique III from the Royal Palace in Madrid

From its origins until today, the Espolón has undergone many reforms. One of the earliest ones was the installation of four statues donated by the king Carlos III, taken from the balustrade of the Royal Palace in Madrid, representing medieval characters related with Burgos: Fernán González, Alfonso XI, Juan I and Enrique III. Four neo-Classical statues were added later on on both ends of the promenade, representing Wamba, Alfonso VI, Juan II and San Millán, donated by Isabel II in 1868. The Salón de Recreo was founded in 1858, and, in 1881, the Círculo de la Unión and several cafés, such as the Café el Suizo.

Protected from the sun by a line of plane trees that replaced the old acacias and lime trees, the Espolón remains the favourite promenade of the people of Burgos.

Puerta de Santa María and Arco de Santa María

Arco de Santa María

Built in the 13th-century walls, the Puerta de Santa María, together with the tower and the arch, are a plastic synthesis of the historical culture that has predominated in Burgos throughout the centuries.

Francisco de Colonia started to build the façade in 1536, on the occasion of the visit of the emperor Carlos I. In order to receive him, and in an attempt to emphasise the social cohesion of the people of Burgos, a monument was designed, featuring the most renowned characters in the history of the city. The monument is dominated by the image of Holy Mary and, below it, the custodian angel of the city, offering religious support to the rest of the images.

The Arco de Santa María features, together for the first time, depictions of the legendary judges of Castile Nuño Rasura (1) and Laín Calvo (2), the symbols of the collective and conciliating spirit of the early times; plus Fernán González (3), count of Castile and head of the Lara family, responsible for the creation of a specifically Castilian territory; Diego Porcelos (4), the founder of the city, El Cid (5), the legendary representative of the eternal values of Castile, and Carlos I (6), the emperor, in the centre of the group, as if fully assuming the ideals of all those around him.

The work was completed by Juan de Vallejo in 1553, with the assistance of Ochoa de Arteaga, who made the statues.

After the reform, it became the actual access gate of the city, which led to a number of refurbishing works in the interior.

Inside is the Sala de Poridad, where the city's Regimiento had its meetings, the mural painting of Fernán González, by the illustrious artist Vela Zanetti, and the Museo de Farmacia, with a pot collection dating from the 17th – 19th centuries.

To end this route, there is a wonderful view of the cathedral from the **Plaza del Rey San Fernando**, commonly known as Plaza del Sarmental. Its origins date back to the 19th century, when the water channels and several bridges were eliminated, and to the early 20th century, when the archbishop's palace, which was attached to the south wall of the cathedral, was demolished.

The city's custodian angel

Plaza del Rey San Fernando

3 Real Monasterio de las Huelgas

The Monasterio de Santa María la Real de las Huelgas forms part of a residential complex founded by Alfonso VIII and Leonor of Aquitaine, to be used as a royal pantheon and the headquarters of the female Cistercian order from 1187.

Real Monasterio de las Huelgas

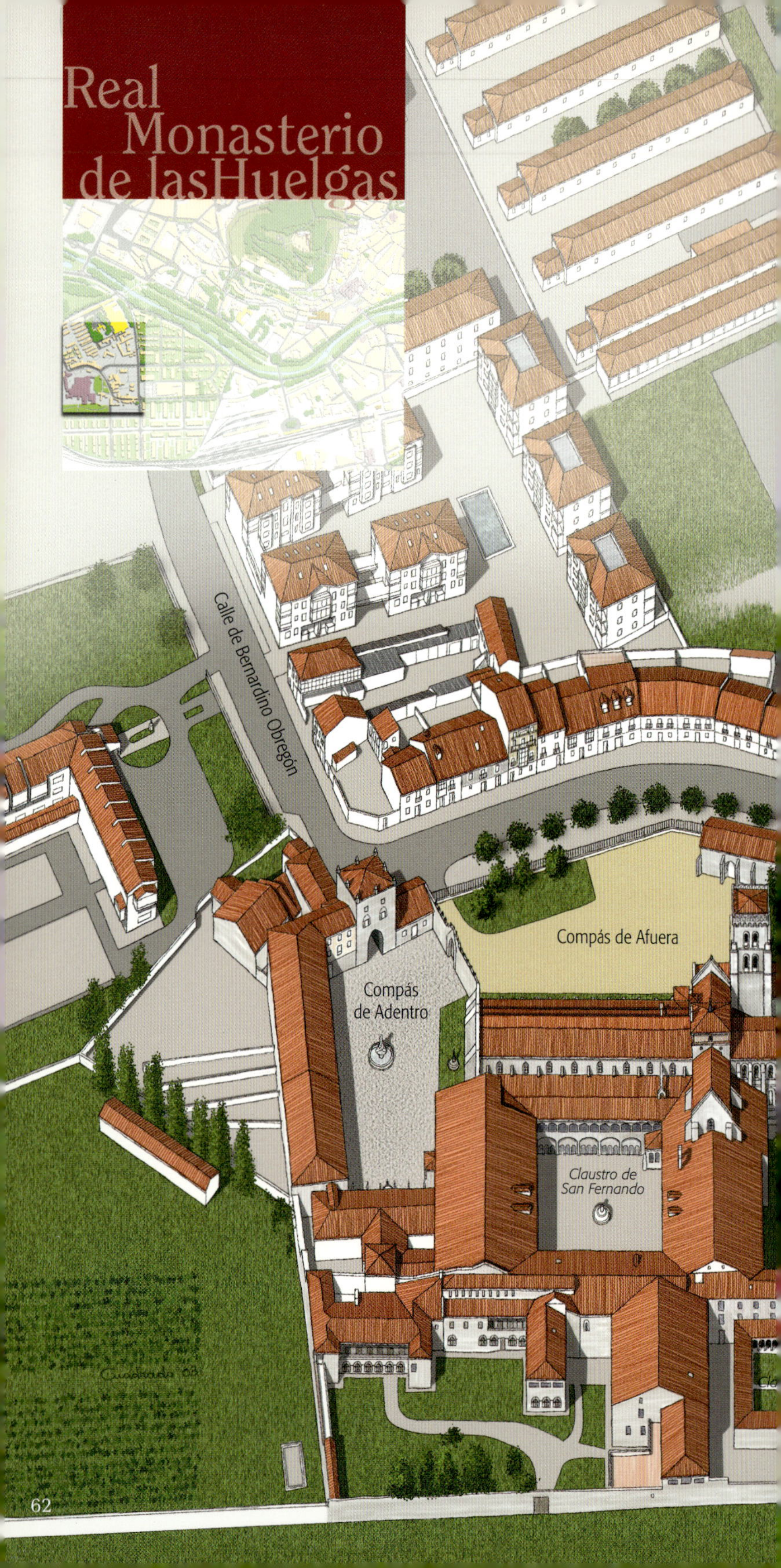

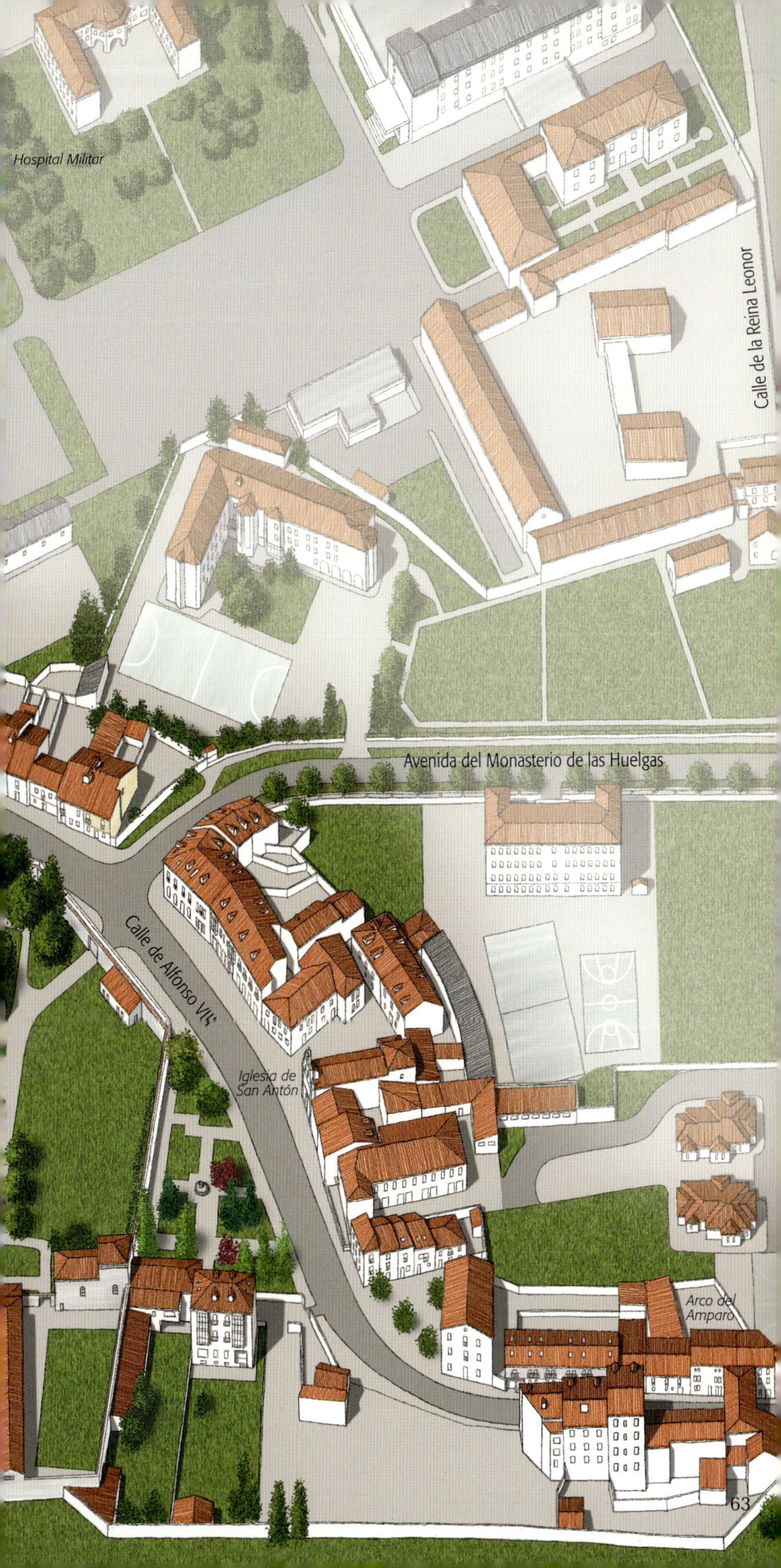
Hospital Militar
Calle de la Reina Leonor
Avenida del Monasterio de las Huelgas
Calle de Alfonso VII
Iglesia de San Antón
Arco del Amparo

Real Monasterio de las Huelgas

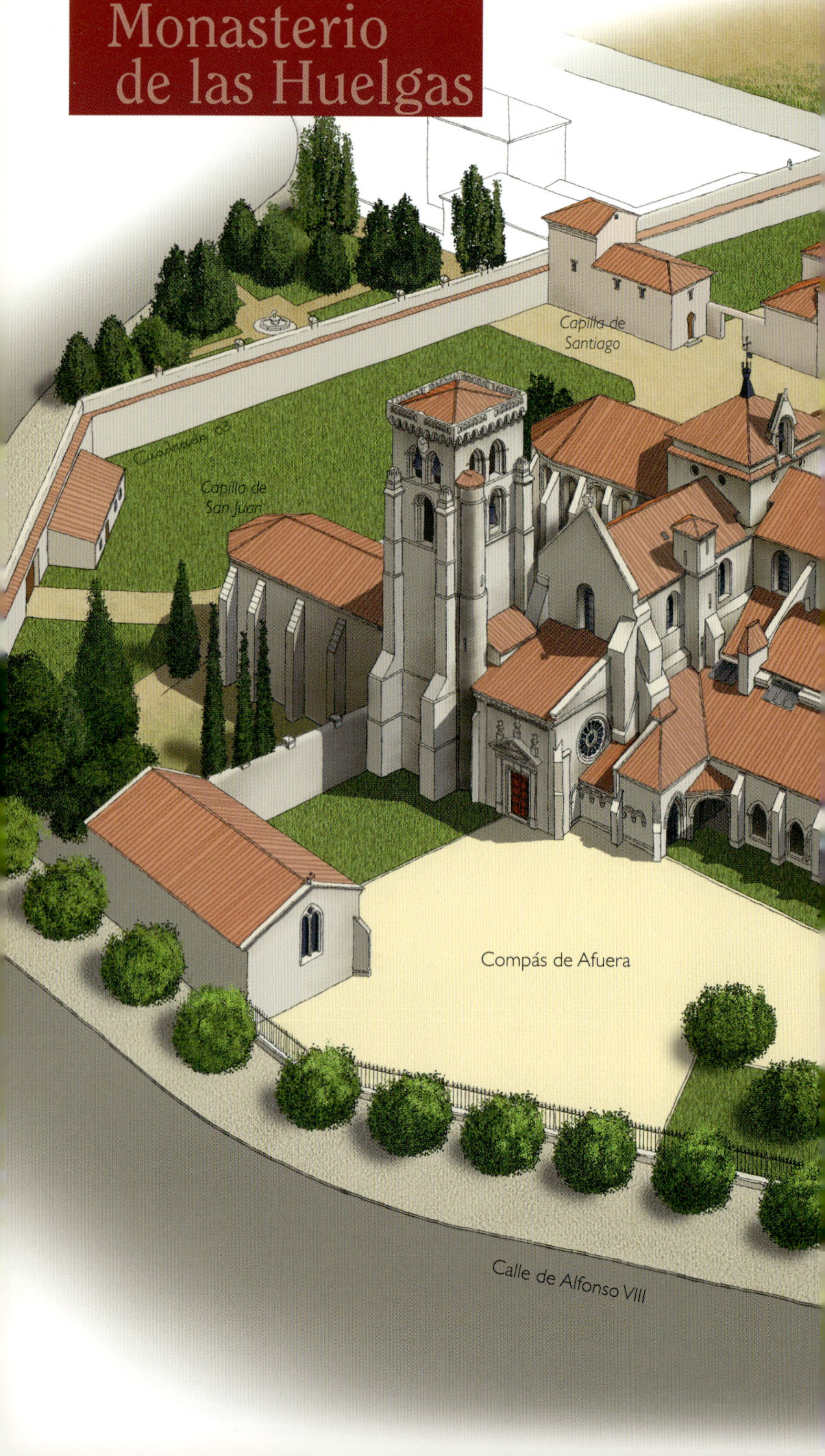

General ground plan of the Real Monasterio de las Huelgas

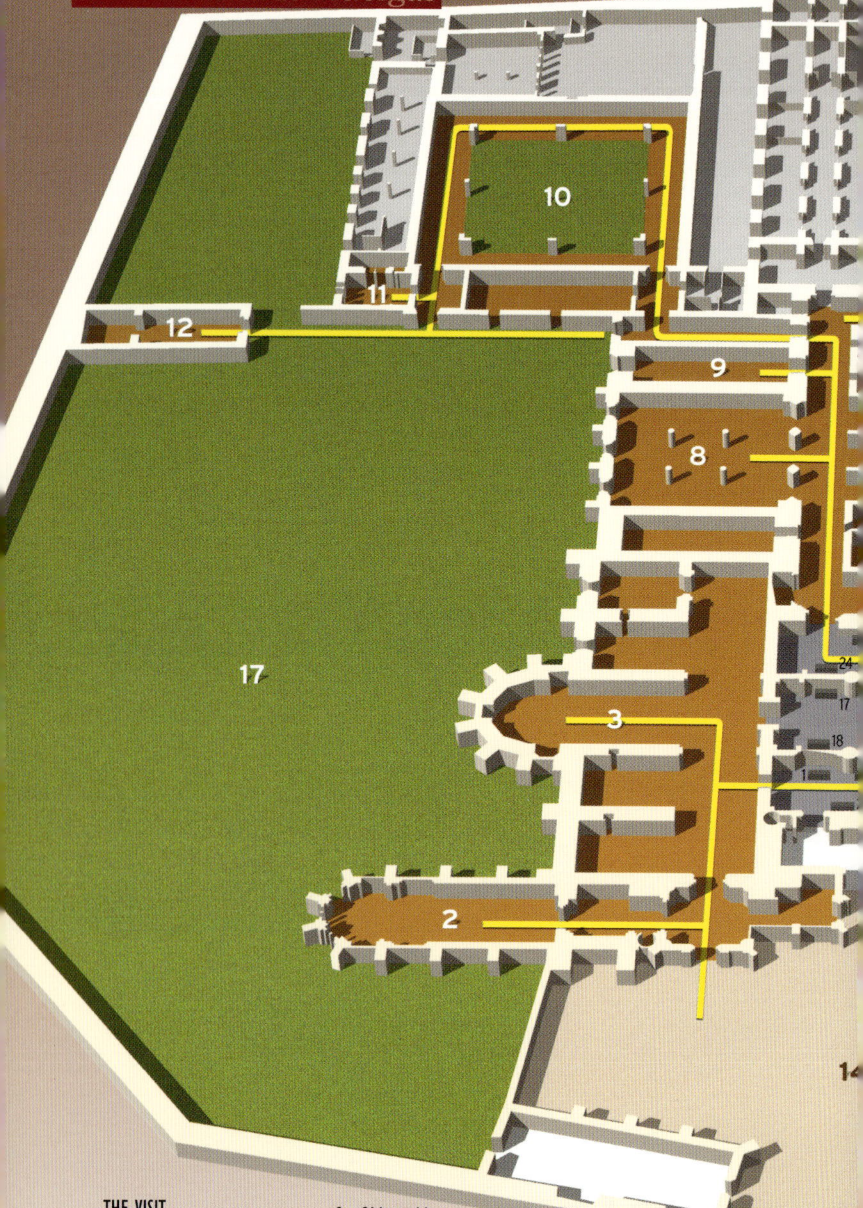

THE VISIT

1 Nave de los Caballeros
2 Capilla de San Juan
3 Altar end
4 Nave de Santa Catalina
5 Main chapel
6 Nave de San Juan
7 Claustro de San Fernando
8 Chapter room
9 Old working room
10 Las Claustrillas
11 Capilla de la Asunción
12 Capilla de Santiago
13 Granary and Museo de Telas Medievales
14 Compás de Afuera
15 Compás de Adentro
16 Porter's office
17 Orchards and garden

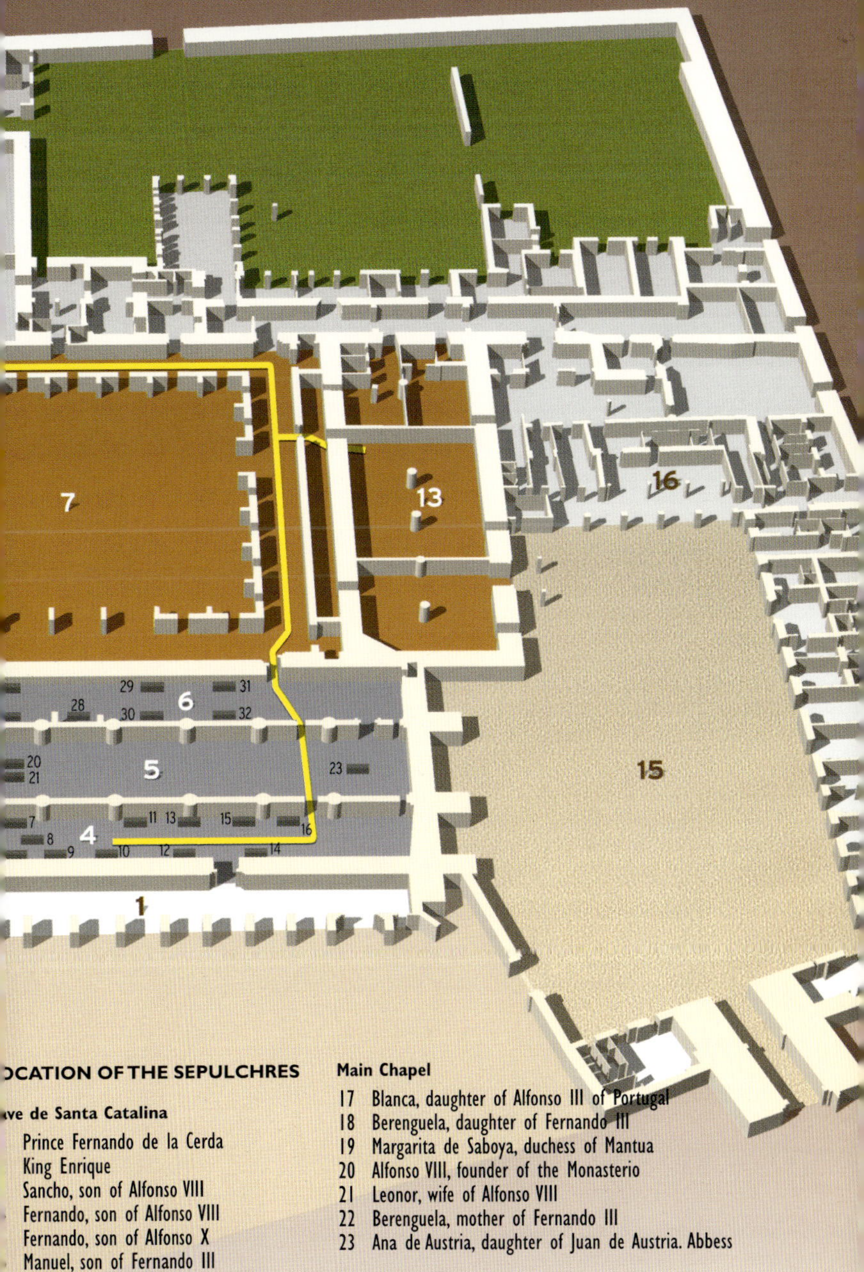

OCATION OF THE SEPULCHRES

ve de Santa Catalina

- Prince Fernando de la Cerda
- King Enrique
- Sancho, son of Alfonso VIII
- Fernando, son of Alfonso VIII
- Fernando, son of Alfonso X
- Manuel, son of Fernando III
- Fernando, son of Sancho IV of Navarra
- Alfonso de la Cerda
- Sancho, son of Alfonso VIII
- Sancha, daughter of Alfonso VIII
- Felipe, son of Sancho IV
- Leonor, daughter of Alfonso VIII
- Leonor, daughter of Alfonso VIII, child
- Sancho, bastard son of Alfonso XI
- Pedro, son of Sancho IV
- Mafalda, daughter of Alfonso VIII

Main Chapel

17 Blanca, daughter of Alfonso III of Portugal
18 Berenguela, daughter of Fernando III
19 Margarita de Saboya, duchess of Mantua
20 Alfonso VIII, founder of the Monasterio
21 Leonor, wife of Alfonso VIII
22 Berenguela, mother of Fernando III
23 Ana de Austria, daughter of Juan de Austria. Abbess

Nave de San Juan

24 Constanza, daughter of Alfonso VIII. Nun.
25 Constanza, daughter of Alfonso IX. Nun.
26 Blanca, daughter of Prince Pedro. Nun.
27 María, daughter of Jaime II
28 Constanza, daughter of Alfonso X. Nun.
29 Isabel de Molina, great-granddaughter of Alfonso IX. Nun.
30 Leonor, daughter of Fernando IV
31 María de Almenar
32 María de Aragón, daughter of Ferdinand the Catholic. Nun.

It was founded by the king Alfonso VIII in 1187, and put under the Cistercian rule. The monarch liked this place so much that he chose it as his and his wife Leonor of Plantagenet's burial ground. Many Castilian ladies lived in it as nuns during the Middle Ages. The abbess had extraordinary religious and jurisdictional powers, and the monastery became one of the most important manors in Castile.

This monastery once held solemn ceremonies, such as the knighting of the kings of Castile Fernando III, Alfonso X, Alfonso XI, Enrique II and Juan I. Even prince Edward, the son of king Henry III of England, was honoured in this fashion in 1255.

The Monasterio de las Huelgas is a complex edifice, with three clearly visible construction stages. The earliest one –late 12th century– corresponds with the further section of the main entrance, and includes the Claustrillas and the Capilla de la Asunción, where the original royal residence must have been located. The expansion works started some years later, and the name of the master Ricardo appears in the documents of that time (1203). The Claustro de San Fernando and the great pre-Gothic monastic church were built in the first third of the 13th century.

There is an impressive view of the whole structure from the **Compás de Afuera**. The three church naves, rising up like a mountain of stone, are topped by the tall tower and the dome. There

is an interesting flying buttress here, a clear indication of the early attempts to implement the new building technologies of the Gothic style. Attached to the north nave is an open atrium-like arcade, with arches and buttresses. This area is known as the Nave de los Caballeros (Nave of the Noblemen), probably because of the large number of Castilian noblemen buried in it. From the Compás de Afuera, the **Compás de Adentro** can be accessed via a pointed arch or through an old tower, where, tradition has it, the king Pedro I was born. This tower must have been part of the network of fortresses, virtually gone today, that protected the monastery and the surrounding area. This yard, or *compás*, contains houses and edifices dating from the 16th and 17th centuries.

The church is accessed via a late 18th-century neo-Classical portal, in the style of the Burgos architect Fernando González de Lara, which opens into the lower part of the tower and leads to the transept. Before entering the temple, you will see a covered space leading, on the one hand, to the **Capilla de San Juan**, an interesting 13th-century structure, and, on the other, to a small room holding a richly decorated pre-Gothic tomb. Light comes into the room through a beautiful eye-shaped window decorated with radius-like paired columns. Past this entrance you will find yourself in the north transept-arm. This may confuse you, since what you see in front of you is not the presbytery but the south side of the transept. The main chapel and the four side ones (two on each side) are to the left, and to the right are the naves that are not visible from this point, since they were mostly blinded in the late 16th century, to preserve the intimacy of the monastery. The **central nave** and the **transept** are the same height, whereas the side

During the knighting ceremony a 13th-century articulate sculpture was used, representing the apostle Saint James, seated, holding a sword in his right hand, which moved by means of an articulate arm, so as to accolade the future knight.

The gabled church front features a combination of vegetal Cistercian elements and heraldic elements concerned with the kingdom of Castile.

Probably the greatest constructive development is to be found at the intersection of the main chapel and the transept, featuring an incipient dome. The pillars separating the naves are simple and octagonal, which gives them a severe appearance.

chapels are much lower. The interior of the temple is simple. Most of the vaults are four-part ribbed vaults, except the one in the presbytery, which has six parts. The **altar end** of the temple is T-shaped. Next to the polygonal central **apse** there are four lower side chapels, two on each side, which, although they have a square ground plan, become octagonal as they rise, due to the introduction of Angers vaults.

In the presbytery, the sobriety of the church architecture turns into an extraordinarily lavish profusion of Baroque decorative motifs. The large **main altarpiece**, perfectly adapted to the architectural structure due to its shell-like topping, is a 1665 work by the assembler Policarpo de la Nestosa and the sculptor Juan de Pobes. The Valladolid painter Pedro Guillerón did the gilding and the polychrome job. Next to Marian scenes and motifs are other scenes dealing with the Cistercian devotion, such as the image of its founder, Saint Bernard, plus some of his miracles and a sculpture of Saint Benedict –the founder of the Benedictine order–, regarded as their first father by the Cistercian order. The complexity of the sculptures and Solomonic columns, together with the brilliancy of the polychrome layer, make this altarpiece one of the most outstanding samples of Baroque sculp-

Miracle of Saint Bernard, main altarpiece

Praying image of Alfonso VIII

Above the door linking the transept with the nave there is a gigantic mural painting by Pedro Ruiz de Camargo, dating from around 1600, representing the founding monarchs, praying, and the battle of Navas de Tolosa (1212), where the Christian troops, including those led by Alfonso VIII, defeated the Muslim almohades.

ture in Burgos. The altarpiece is continued, on the sides, by two facing cenotaphiums containing the praying sculptures of the founders of the monastery. It is interesting to note that the actual sculptures, carved by Juan de Pobes at the same time as the altarpiece, are anachronistic in the sense that their clothes seem to date from the 17th century. Further down, on the presbytery wall to your right, stands the convent's great 18th-century organ. On both sides of this space are the chaplains' stalls, carved by the carpenter Enrique del Rey in the mid 17th century, in contrast with the rest of the furniture of the presbytery, since they are not painted. Right opposite the altarpiece is an accessway connecting the transept and the lower end of the main chapel, through which the nuns could attend the offices held at the main altar.

Through a small door in the north transept-arm you will reach the **north nave**, devoted to Saint Catherine, containing some interesting tombs of the royal family. Of particular interest is the tomb of Fernando de la Cerda (1275), decorated with a fine gable and presided by a Calvary. This was the only sepulchre left unspoilt by the Napoleonic hordes, and the rich bridal dowry that was found inside can be seen today in the monastery's Museo de Telas. The sarcophagus has an interesting painted heraldic decoration. Next to this sepulchre are other more plain ones, such as the tomb of Enrique I, the ill-starred son of Alfonso VIII, who was killed by a roof tile when he was a child. When this tomb was opened, in the mid 20th century, it was found that the young

The chapel next to the main chapel holds a 16th-century altarpiece, featuring a beautiful Renaissance sculpture of Christ on the Cross by Diego de Siloe.

Sepulchre of Berenguela

Sepulchre of the prince Alfonso de la Cerda

monarch had been subjected to trepanation in an attempt to heal his wounds. This nave also contains the small tomb of Leonor or Sancho, and that of Alfonso de la Cerda, dating from the early and the late 13th century, respectively.

The **main chapel** is presided by the paired sarcophaguses, with two-sided covers, of the founders Alfonso VIII and Leonor of Plantagenet, dating from the early 13th century. Leaning against recumbent lions, they are decorated with Castilian (the castles) and Plantagenet (crowned leopards and passing animals) heraldic motifs. The sarcophagus of the king features, on its upper end,

Main chapel

Attached to the wall separating the transept from this nave is an interesting altarpiece-baldachin dating from the early 16th century, supporting a splendid and theatrical group of sculptures dating from the late 13th or the early 14th centuries, representing the Descent from the Cross.

the figure of the king handing the foundational bull to the community of Cistercian nuns. The tomb of the queen features a Calvary. In this area, around the royal tombs, are the most outstanding burial monuments of the monastery. Particularly noteworthy is the sepulchre of Berenguela, which had been originally designed for her grandmother, the queen of the same name and daughter of the founders, who, in an act of modesty, requested to be buried in the ground. It is richly decorated with scenes of

Sepulchre of Alfonso VIII and Leonor, founders of the monastery

the Childhood of Christ, the Coronation of the Virgin and the death and translation to Heaven of the deceased. Opposite stands the tomb of Blanca de Guimaraes (†1321), the daughter of the Portuguese king Sancho III and his wife Beatriz, the daughter of Alfonso X. The nuns' stalls, dating from the 17th century, are extremely plain, in line with the Cistercian sobriety. Next to the abbess' chair, on the south side, beside the royal tombs, is the abbess' staff, the symbol of monastic authority. The lower end of the main chapel was transformed in the early 17th century. At the request of the abbess Ana of Austria, the daughter of the winner of the Battle of Lepanto, a chapel was built there, where she lies buried, surrounded by a wooden screen featuring the sculpted figures of her relatives and ancestors. The altarpiece of the chapel has some sculptures from the late 16th-century altarpiece by Juan de Anchieta.

The **south nave**, devoted to Saint John, is presided by an altarpiece, made with the remains of other 16th-century altarpieces, featuring an interesting Gothic Calvary. Then you will reach the

Also very interesting is the beautiful Mudejar doorway at the beginning of the eastern side of the cloister, which must have been built in the early 13th century.

Mudéjar plasterwork, Claustro de San Fernando

The Chapter Room of the monastery is an elegant Gothic structure containing paintings dating from the 15th, 16th and 17th centuries, some of them of Flemish origin, and the famous Pendón de las Navas de Tolosa, a Muslim work of the early 13th century, which rather than a heraldic emblem must have been part of the tent of the Muslim king, taken during the battle of Navas de Tolosa and traditionally regarded as one of the most peculiar war relics in Castile.

Chapter Room

Claustro de San Fernando. Built in the early 13th century, its arcades were blinded in the late 18th century, in order to protect the interior from the cold and reinforce the structure, since new monastic rooms were being built on the upper level. The four corridors are covered with pointed barrel vaults featuring traces of the old 1250 Mudéjar plasterwork, representing beautiful vegetal, animal, geometric and heraldic motifs. In the angle parts of the cloister this decoration was replaced in 1500.

The most interesting cloister room is the **Chapter Room**, a singular architectural space, covered by nine ribbed vaults resting on four pillars with drum-shaped capitals and small monolithic columns.

On the west side of the cloister is a spacious room that was once used as the grain barn of the monastery and which, today, is being restored and will be one of the rooms of the **Museo de Telas**. The collection of tomb fabrics is one of the best

Museo de Telas

of its class in Europe, representing a superb synthesis of the oriental influences and the Christian decorative styles.

Past the Claustro de San Fernando, and through a long corridor, you will reach the **Capilla de Santiago**, with 13th-century Mudéjar elements, although its most outstanding feature is the superb 15th-century Moorish artesonado ceiling. From this point you can also access the **Claustrillas**, one of the oldest areas of the monastery. It is a late Gothic cloister, with stylised vegetal Cistercian capitals and round arches. Next to this cloister is

Las Claustrillas

Las Claustrillas. It has already been pointed out that the almohade Capilla de la Asunción might have been a room of the palace attached to the original monastery, although recent research indicates that this space was the *qubba* or centralised burial ground of some important palace character.

the so-called **Capilla de la Asunción**, an interesting early 13th-century room; the Muslim master builders at the service of the monarch left good evidence of their skills in this refined and exquisite work. Today, the chapel is presided by a 13th-century Gothic stone sculpture of Our Lady of Las Huelgas. There is an area not opened to visitors in the cloister, featuring some extremely interesting spaces, such as the **Capilla del Salvador**, an important 13th-century Mudéjar structure. You must get a permit from the Patrimonio Nacional if you wish to visit this area.

Capilla de la Asunción

4

Museo de Burgos

The Museo de Burgos, located in the houses of Miranda, Iñigo Angulo and the Casa de Melgosa, three fundamental samples of Burgos Renaissance civil architecture, is a magnificent showcase of the enormous creativity of the inhabitants of this land from the Palaeolithic until today. Visiting the museum is a wonderful way to get to know, in a summarised manner, the history and the art of Burgos and its province.

Museo de Burgos

Page 118

Page 107

Page 119

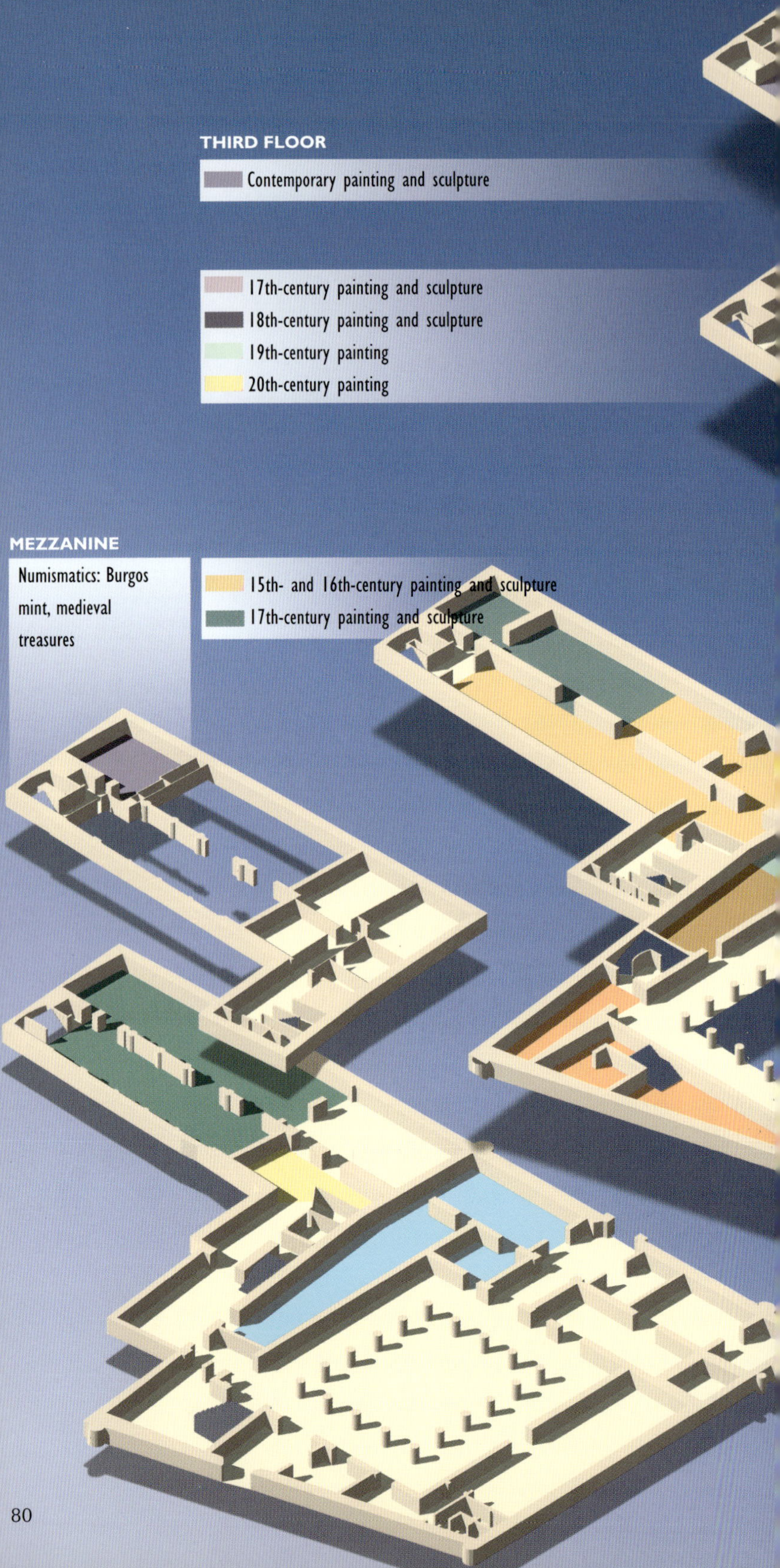
THIRD FLOOR
Contemporary painting and sculpture
17th-century painting and sculpture
18th-century painting and sculpture
19th-century painting
20th-century painting
MEZZANINE
Numismatics: Burgos mint, medieval treasures
15th- and 16th-century painting and sculpture
17th-century painting and sculpture

Museo de Burgos

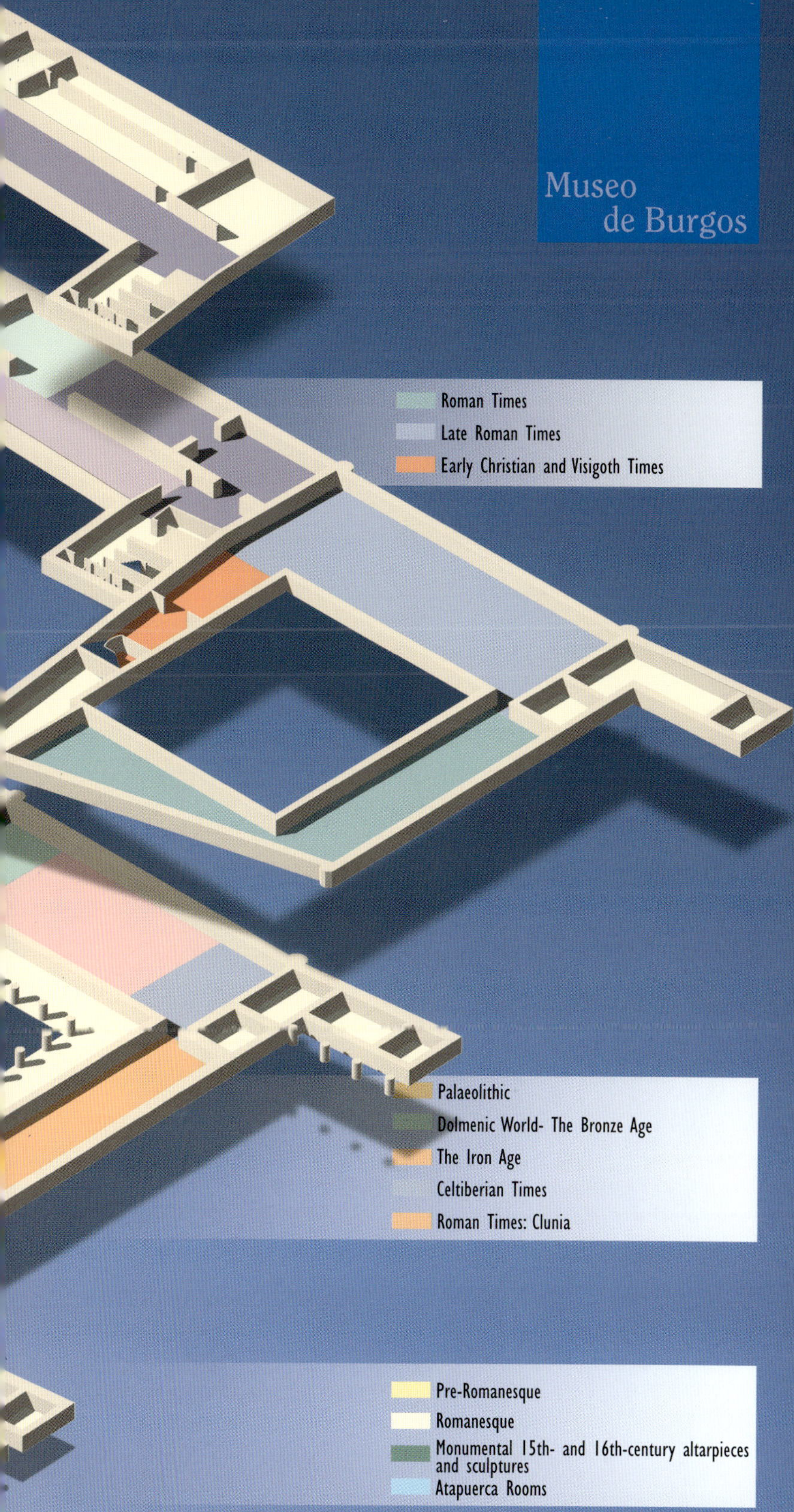

*The **Museo de Burgos** was founded in 1846 as a custody and exhibition centre for the art objects collected by the State on occasion of the sale of the Church lands carried out by Mendizábal in the province of Burgos. Originally, the Museo was located in the old Seminario de San Jerónimo, in the Convento de las Trinas, and in the Arco de Santa María. In 1955 the collection was transferred to the Casa de Miranda. The new premises of the museum's archaeological section were opened in 1983, and the fine arts section, in the adjacent Casa de Íñigo Angulo, in 1990. Shortly the museum will be extended in the Casa de Melgosa.*

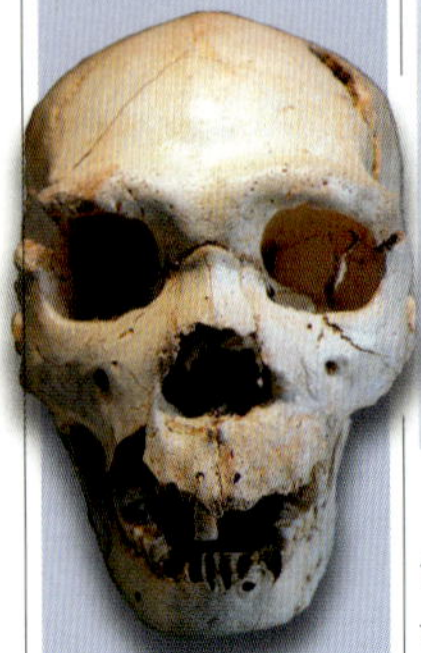

Atapuerca skull

The **pre-history and archaeological section**, located in the Casa de Miranda (7), opens with a general view of the most remote history of the province of Burgos. Here you will find archaeological and paleontological remnants from the nearby sites of the Sierra de Atapuerca, such as the outstanding human fossils, 800,000 to 250,000 years old. Next to them are stone artefacts such as bifaces, triedrums and knives from the sites near the capital. There are also some very interesting collections of Neolithic and Bronze Age pieces. Particularly noteworthy are the artefacts found during the excavation of some dolmens and necropolis such as Cubillejo de Lara, Villalmanzo and

Patio

Mosaic of Cardeñajimeno, detail

Bronze Age Fable

Early Christian sepulchre

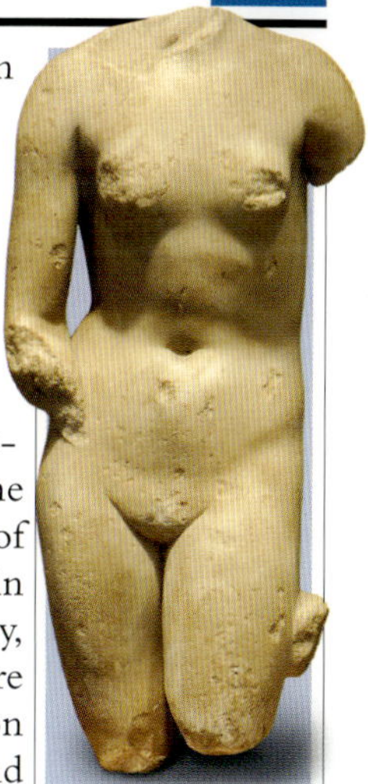
Roman Venus

the Cerro de San Miguel. The remains found in the Polera necropolis in Ubierna and in other necropolis, such as Villanueva de Teba and Miraveche, are among the most interesting ever found. The Roman era is superbly represented by a wide variety of pieces from important sites, such as Clunia, located in Peñalba de Castro. A magnificent collection of pottery, stone sculptures and the remnants of mosaic works are among the most interesting artefacts found in relation with the romanisation process. The early Christian and Visigothic era left some interesting objects, such as the illustrated sarcophaguses of Bureba and the remains of liturgical dowries found around the hermitage of Quintanilla de las Viñas.

The Casa de Íñigo Angulo (7) houses the museum's **fine arts section**. The visit starts with a series of archaeological remains dating from the 8th - 11th centuries, most of them found in the old monastic centres of the

Frontal de Silos

province of Burgos. Of the old Ermita de las Santas Elena y Centola, in Valdeteja, have been preserved some architectural structures and an altar table. Also very interesting is the rich collection of stele dating from the late 8th to the 10th centuries. The Romanesque period is superbly represented by a series of unique internationally known pieces, such as the Frontal de Silos, dating from 1170. Also of note are the 10th-century ivory case made in the workshops of Medina Azahara and the Muslim chest from the workshops of Cuenca, made in 1026 and decorated with Christian enamels in the 12th century. Next to these artefacts you will also find some enamelled

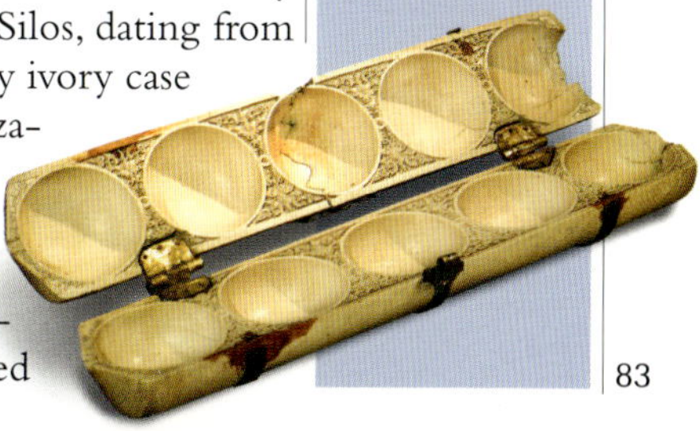
Muslim case

chests from the workshops of Limoges, probably dating from the 12th century.

Recently, the Museo de Burgos acquired the statue of the Virgen de las Batallas (Virgin of Battles), an interesting enamelled sculpture-reliquary from the Monasterio de San Pedro de Arlanza. Of the Gothic period stand out the 14th-century funereal sculptures of noblemen found in Villasandino, the large Hispano-Flemish altarpiece of San Pedro de Tejada, by Alonso de Zamora, the painted Passion fabrics of the Monasterio de Oña, made by the same artist around 1500, the late 15th-century tomb of Juan de Padilla, by Gil de Siloe, and the statue of the Virgin from the Arco de Santa María, by the master of Covarrubias.

The Museo has a good collection of 16th-century Flemish paintings, such as the board painting of the Burial of Christ, by Isembrandt, and the Ecce Homo by Mossart. Of the Renaissance period stand out the board painting of the Mass of Saint Gregory, by Pedro de

Virgen de las Batallas

Mass of Saint Gregory in the altarpiece of San Pedro de Tejada

Sepulchre of Juan de Padilla

Virgin, Arco de Santa María

Altarpiece, Monasterio de Vileña

Berruguete, the sculpture of Jesus as a Child, by Miguel Ángel Nacherino, the panels of the old altarpiece of La Merced in Burgos, carved by Gregorio Pardo in the mid 16th century, and the Romanist 1580 altarpiece of the Monasterio de Vileña, by Pedro López de Gámiz.

The Baroque years are represented by paintings by local masters such as Mateo Cerezo the Younger. Among the most interesting canvas paintings of this period is one of Alonso de San Vitores, painted by Juan Rizi in 1659; its background features a crepuscular view of the city of Burgos. The 19th century includes an interesting series of works by local painters such as Dióscoro Puebla, García Prieto, Antonio Cortés and Isidro Gil. The fine arts section also includes works by contemporary Burgos masters, such as Vela Zanetti, Muñoz Melgosa, Ciruelos, Luis Sáez, Carazo or Ignacio del Río, representing the different pictorial trends of the 20th century.

The Museo de Burgos also has a superb Collection of Decorative and Industrial Arts, including some outstanding pieces, such as a coin collection featuring all the coins minted at the Burgos mint and the remains of the Jewish treasure of Briviesca. Also of interest are the furniture, such as the chairs and bargueño desks, exhibited in this section.

Treasure of Briviesca

Portrait of brother Alonso de San Vitores

Martyrdom of Saint John the Baptist by Dióscoro Puebla

Dream, by Luis Sáez

5 Cartuja de Miraflores

The Real Cartuja de Miraflores is one of the most interesting art structures of the late Gothic period. This building, mostly erected under Isabel the Catholic as a pantheon for her parents, the king Juan II and the queen Isabel of Portugal, holds some of the most remarkable sculptures of the 15th century, combining ample forms with a complex iconographic content.

Cartuja de Miraflores

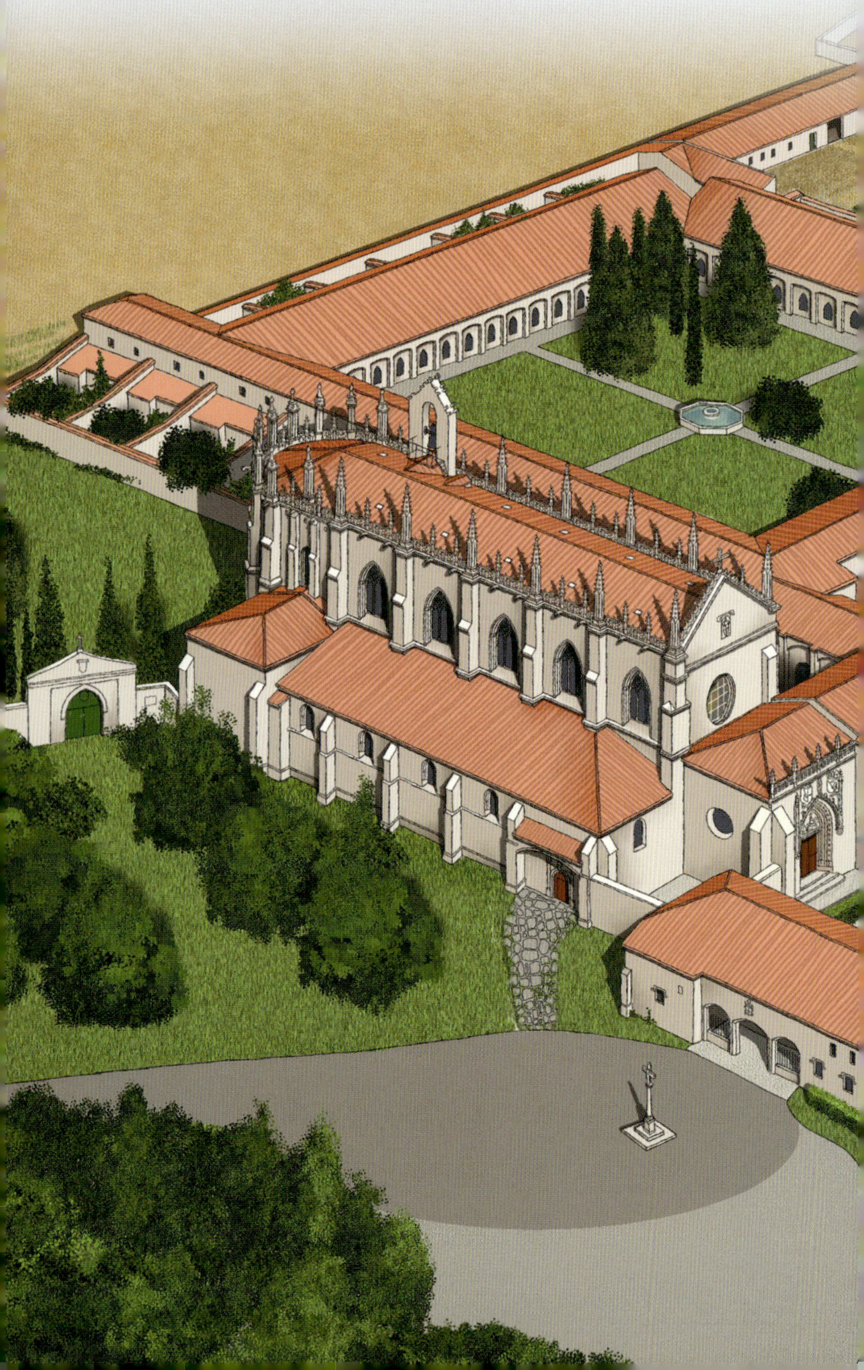

Cuadrado

General ground plan of the Cartuja de Miraflores

ARTISTIC ELEMENTS

1 Church Gate
2 Coro de Legos Stalls
3 Coro de Padres Stalls
4 Sepulchre of Juan II of Castile and Isabel of Portugal
5 Main Altarpiece
6 Flemish Triptych
7 Annunciation by Pedro de Berruguete
8 Sepulchre of prince Alfonso
9 Image of San Bruno, by Manuel Pereira
10 18th-century mural paintings

AREAS

A Church Atrium
B Room for the faithful
C Coro de los Legos
D Coro de Padres
E Presbytery
F Capilla de San Bruno
G Capilla de Nuestra Señora de Mi
H Capilla de las Reliquias

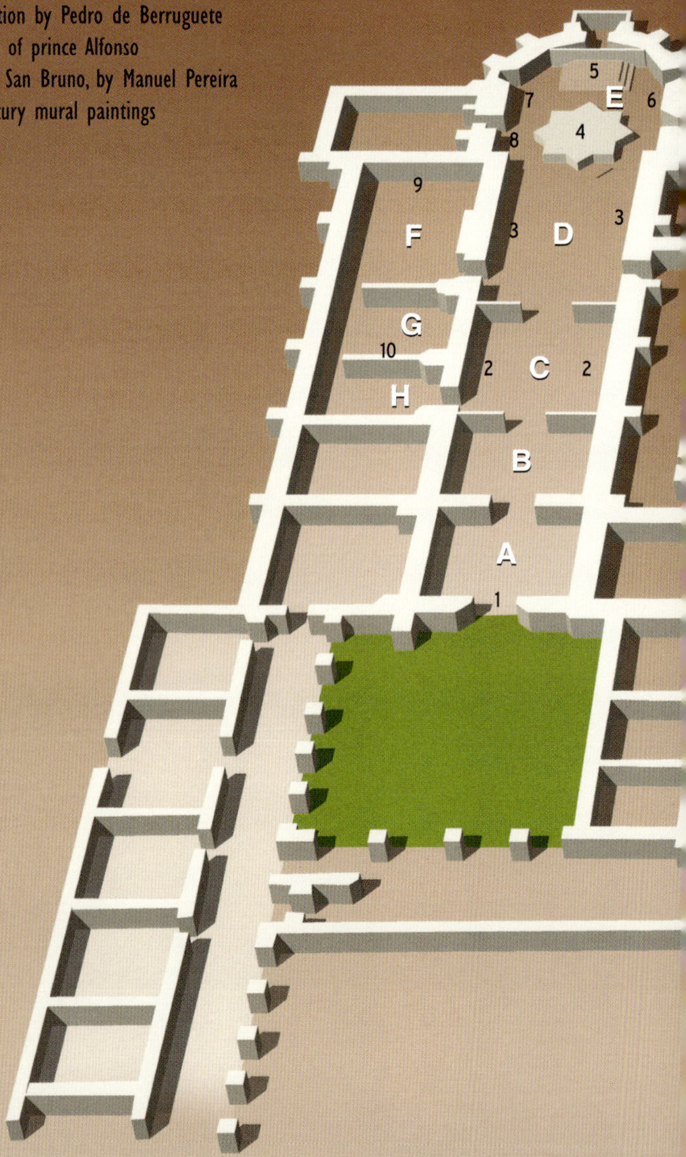

In 1401 the king Enrique III founded a small palace-fortress surrounded by a large park where the king used to take strolls and relax. This building soon became known as Miraflores, since that was the traditional name of the land where it stood. Nothing is known of the features of that early structure. In 1441 Juan II, the son of Enrique III, decided to build a convent on the site of the old country estate, thus complying with the wish of his father. Although, in his will, the king had said that the monastery was to be occupied by the Franciscan order, his son Juan decided to give it to the Carthusians.

In 1452, when the refurbishing works of the fortress were still in progress, a fire burnt everything to the ground. This disastrous accident did not discourage the king, who commissioned Juan de Colonia to reconstruct it in 1454. The king died in Valladolid after the works had started, and a provisional sepulchre was installed in the new Cartuja. The works were interrupted during the convulsive years of the kingdom of Enrique IV.

The situation changed when Isabel the Catholic came to power and the monarchy became more stable. In 1483, after visiting the pantheon where the mortal remains of her father

were kept, which was in a deplorable condition, the queen decided to resume the works, and commissioned the architect Garci Fernández de Matienzo and Simon de Colonia, the son of the master builder who had started the works almost thirty years back, to complete the Cartuja. Closely supervised by the queen herself, the works pushed on and were finished in 1488.
The plan of the Catholic queen was to erect an impressive, dynastic mausoleum, honouring his parents and his brother, the Infante Alfonso, who had been proclaimed king by the belligerent nobility in detriment of his brother Enrique IV. This way, she intended to erase the memory of this king and emphasise the dynastic continuity through the figure of Juana la Beltraneja.

The founder's coat of arms

The structure of the Cartuja is typical of the Carthusian order: a single-nave church with the cells orbiting surrounding a large cloister. Garci Fernández de Matienzo and Simón de Colonia preserved the ground plan designed by Juan de Colonia. The architectural complex is dominated by the church, which features flamboyant Gothic windows between buttresses and a polygonal apse. The Renaissance capitals and the crenellations topping the structure were added in 1539 by the sculptor Diego de Mendieta. Access to this church is via a hall leading to a first yard containing the **main portal**, which features large-scale reproductions of the coats of arms of Juan II supported by large lions. The door, decorated with a beautiful ogee arch flanked by two capitals, features a tympanum with the expressive image of the Pietà. Above it, a large eye-shaped window lets light into the temple. A pediment tops the façade, where an angel holds the arms of the Catholic Queen.

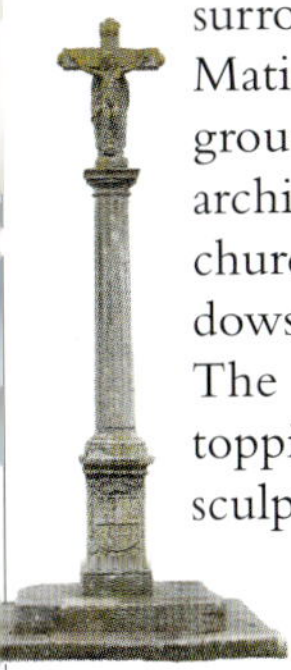

Pietá in the front's tympanum

Since the time of the Catholic Queen, this Carthusian church has held many important events. In it was temporarily buried Felipe the Handsome, the husband of Juana the Mad, until she decided to exhume him and take his mortal remains to Granada. Visiting the Cartuja was a must for many of the kings arriving in Burgos. The Napoleonic invasion brought about the dispersion of part of the art collections of the Cartuja, and the magnificent altarpiece of Saint John, painted by Juan de Flandes in the late 15th century, was stolen.

The sale of the Church lands forced the Carthusian community to leave the building, although, fortunately, most of the moveable property was conserved. After temporarily housing a leper hospital and a Casa de Venerables (nursing home for old priests), it was returned to the community in 1880, resuming religious activity with the affection of the people of Burgos.

The Legos stalls are by Simón de Bueras. They were carved in 1558. They feature a rich iconographic programme including saints and the founders of religious orders on the backs and scenes of the life of Christ on the tops.

Through this door you will reach the atrium, covered by a large star vault featuring multiple heraldic and epigraphic elements related with the founding monarchs.

Vault

The **church** is illuminated by means of large stained-glass windows brought in from Flanders by the Burgos merchant Martín de Soria. The temple is divided into two Carthusian spaces devoted to the novice or convert brethren and to the fathers. Access to the former is via the grille that separates the public space from the convent, partly built by Francisco de Salamanca in 1493. The **Coro de Legos** contains wonderful stalls, on both sides of the nave.

From here, the novice brethren could access the main cloister by crossing a beautiful Renaissance gate featuring fine stone carvings representing the Evangelists and the Four Fathers of the Church. In order to access the fathers' choir, you must cross a partition of sorts consisting of two large 17th-century altarpieces by Policarpo de la Nestosa, featuring two large paintings representing the Adoration of the Magi and the Holy Family. In the centre, a gate topped by sculptures of the Immaculate and two angels, carved by the Baroque Rioja sculptor Bernardo de Elcarreta, leads to the next church space. An inscription saying *Felix Porta Coeli* marks this entrance and relates the Virgin with the gate of salvation.

Holy Family. 17th century altarpiece

The **Coro de Padres** features impressive 1489 choir stalls by Martín Sánchez de Valladolid.

This choir also leads to the cloister through a small pointed gate with a tympanum featuring a15th-century alabaster image of the seated Virgin holding the Child Jesus, by Gil de Siloe.

In the presbytery, the simple vaults at the lower end of the temple are richly de-

Coro de Padres. Stalls

corated with the Angers motifs typical of the style of Simón de Colonia. This is a way to mark the most important room of this church, occupied by the presbytery and a number of sepulchres. The main wall is occupied by the large **altarpiece** made by Gil de Siloe

The Coro de Padres consists of forty walnut stalls, all of them crowned by a running canopy richly decorated with conopial and flaming motifs. Of particular interest are the two backs where the sculptor let his imagination fly, achieving an unrestrained display of geometric motifs, all of them different from one another, showing a Mudéjar influence. Next to the presbytery is the priest's ceremonial chair, topped by an impressive capital, and the lectern, both of them stylistically and chronologically similar to the stalls in the Coro de Padres.

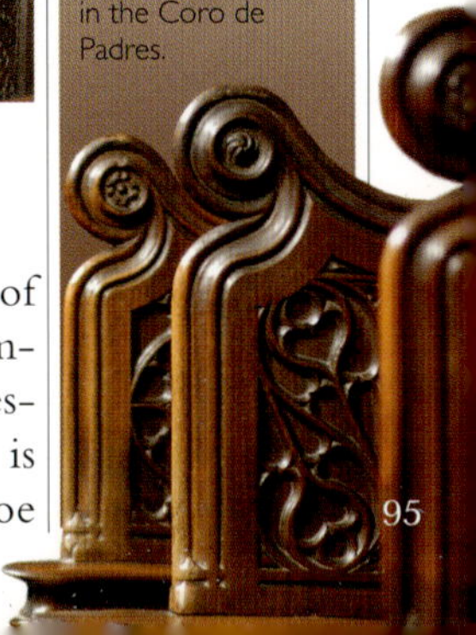

between 1496 and 1499, with the collaboration of Diego de la Cruz, responsible for the gilding and polychrome job. It is a variegated tapestry-like work, with a large circular host-like element made of angels, containing a figure of Christ crucified and dead. Above it is the figure of a pelican feeding its own flesh to its chickens, a clear reference to the sacrifice of Christ and the Eucharist. The cross is supported by God and the Holy Ghost, the latter being represented with unusual anthropomorphic characters. The free spaces of the circle are filled with four scenes of the Passion. Tangential to this circular element are four other circles with the figures of the Evangelists, the empty spaces being filled with sculptures of the Four Fathers of the Church. Saint Peter and Saint Paul flank the main complex. On the outside and at the top of the altarpiece there is a series of small images of saints venerated by the Carthusian order.

On the large altarpiece bench there are four scenes of the life of Christ: the Annunciation, the Adoration of the Magi, the Last Supper, featuring Mary Magdalene kneeled before Christ –combining two passages of the Gospel into a single scene– and the Arrest of Christ. Four large statues of Saint Catheri-

Last Supper at the base of the main altarpiece

Representation of the Holy Trinity, main altarpiece

Holy Ghost

Praying figure of Juan II accompanied by Saint James at the base of the main altarpiece

ne, Saint John the Baptist, Mary Magdalene and Saint James show the main personal devotions of the monarchs. In the central part of the bench stands the 17th-century tabernacle-exhibitor and, right above it, a niche that, depending of the liturgical time of the year, contains a different scene.

In front of the altarpiece, occupying most of the presbytery, is the magnificent alabaster **tomb of the monarchs** Juan II and Isabel of Portugal, built by Gil de Siloe between 1489 and 1493. It is one of the most interesting pieces of European funereal art in the late Middle Ages. It is shaped like a tumulus and features an

Sepulchre of Juan II and Isabel of Portugal

Isabel of Portugal and Juan II

innovative eight-point star ground plan. A complex architectural structure supports a notable group of sculptures. In the upper level are the recumbent, but not dead, figures of the monarchs, two large statues on stands covered with a canopy. They are wearing the elegant clothes of the court, decorated with rich brocades with precious stones. The king is holding a staff with his right hand, a symbol of royal power, and the queen is reading a book of hours. It is a good idea to climb the stairs of the presbytery to contemplate these two effigies correctly.

The walls of the tumulus are decorated with sculptures of the kings of Israel, in clear reference to the divine origins of the monarchy, and of the Virtues, a clear reference to the qualities that rulers must have. Next to these images are the figures of the prophets, of characters of the Old Testament, an image of the Virgin and Child, and several royal escutcheons.

And there is still another interesting group of sculptures in the presbytery area: the tomb of the Infante Alfonso, also by Gil de Siloe. It is a rich arcosolium, containing the praying figure of the prince looking at the altarpiece. The tomb features a profusion of cardines, combining figures of children and animals. At the top of the ogee

The king David in the sepulchre of the kings

Sepulchre of the prince Alfonso

Saint Thomas

One of the most interesting sculptures to be found in the lower section of this sepulchre is that of Saint Thomas, which some scholars have interpreted as the artist's self-portrait.

arch are the image of Saint Michael and the scene of the Annunciation.

The main altarpiece of the Cartuja and these two sepulchres are, without a doubt, one of the most outstanding sets of late Gothic European sculpture, showing the elegance and aesthetic sophistication reached by the Burgos Gothic style before diluting itself into the new Renaissance forms.

Annunciation by Pedro de Berruguete

Two interesting paintings are kept in the presbytery area: the large 15th-century Flemish triptych, with the Crucifixion as its main motif, and the exceptional 1500 board painting of the Annunciation, by Pedro Berruguete, showing, more clearly than any other work, the inertial survival of a series of Gothic elements in a space dominated by typically Renaissance forms.

A door on the north side of the presbytery leads to the **Capilla de San Bruno**, featuring a Renaissance altarpiece containing the beautiful and devout image of the founder of the Carthusian Order, carved by Manuel Pereira, a Madrid-based Portuguese sculptor, in the se-

Image of San Bruno, by Manuel Pereira

cond quarter of the 17th century. It was a donation of the cardinal Antonio Zapata, a great benefactor of the order. This chapel, in turn, leads to the Capilla de la Virgen de Miraflores, featuring an expressive 18th-century Baroque mural painting, with a variety of Marian emblems, inspired by the book *Flores de Miraflores* (Flowers of Miraflores), written by the Burgos Carthusian friar Nicolás de la Iglesia. Finally, you will reach the **Capilla de la Compasión**, with an altarpiece-reliquary brought from Flanders in the late 16th century, plus early Renaissance board paintings representing scenes of the History of the Holy Cross.

Altarpiece of San Bruno

Many other works of art are to be found in the enclosed area of the Cartuja de Miraflores, such as the gilded silver chalice presented by Juan II, the board painting of the late 15th-century Ecce Homo by Juan de Flandes, and a series of interesting paintings dating from the 16th -18th centuries, among which stand out the ones by Diego de Leiva, a Carthusian artist, who lived within these walls in the 17th century.

Adoration of the Cross, Maestro de Santa Cruz

Mural paintings, Capilla de la Virgen de Miraflores

6 The medieval town

The Middle Ages left a deep mark in the city by the Arlanzón. Its present urban layout, the organisation of open spaces, the occupation of the built-up areas are those of the 10th-15th centuries. What is left today is the skeleton of an imaginary, hidden medieval town on the castle hillsides, and a more undefined one, on the plain, deeply transformed by urban activity during the 19th century.

The medieval town

Page 118

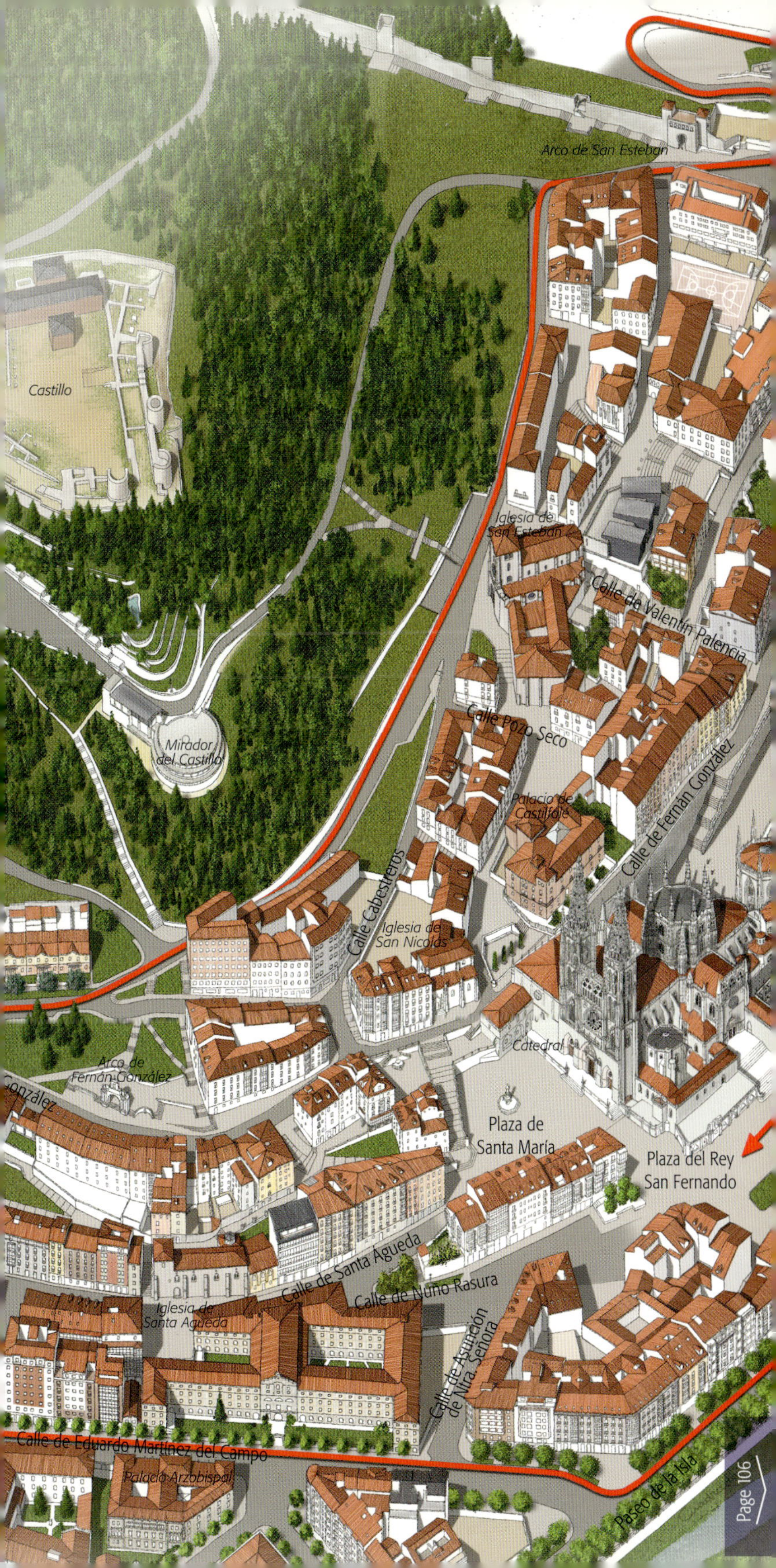
Arco de San Esteban
Castillo
Iglesia de San Esteban
Calle de Valentín Palencia
Calle Pozo Seco
Mirador del Castillo
Palacio de Castilfalé
Calle de Fernán González
Calle Cabestreros
Iglesia de San Nicolás
Catedral
Arco de Fernán González
González
Plaza de Santa María
Plaza del Rey San Fernando
Calle de Santa Águeda
Calle de Nuño Rasura
Iglesia de Santa Águeda
Calle de Asunción de Ntra. Señora
Calle de Eduardo Martínez del Campo
Palacio Arzobispal
Paseo de la Isla
Page 106

Calle de las Corazas
Arco de San Gil
Iglesia de San Gil
Calle de San Gil
Calle de Avellanos
Calle del Hospital de los Ciegos
Calle de Fernán González
Arco del Pilar
Calle del San Lorenzo
Iglesia de San Lorenzo
Plaza de los Castaños
Casa del Cubo
Plaza del Huerto del Rey
Calle de Laín Calvo
Calle del Almirante Bonifaz
Llana de Afuera
Llana de Adentro
Calle del Cardenal Segura
Pasaje del Mercado
Plaza Mayor
C/. Carnicerías
Calle Sombrerería
Calle de la Virgen de la Paloma
Ayuntamiento
Paseo del Espolón
Paseo de Marceliano Santa María
Arco de Santa María
Río Arlanzón
Puente de Santa María
Calle de Valladolid
Plaza de Vega

Page 105

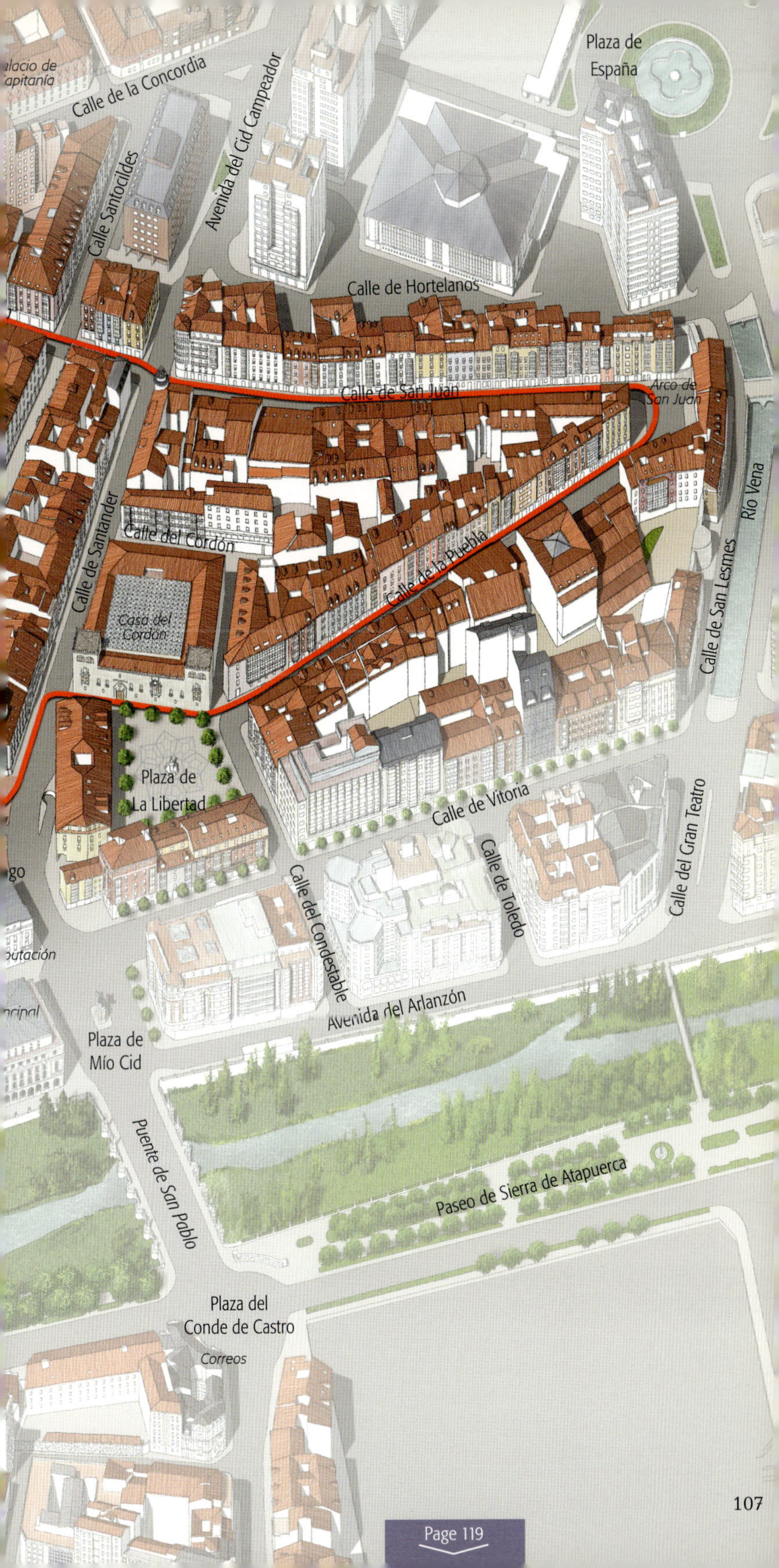
alacio de
apitanía
Calle de la Concordia
Avenida del Cid Campeador
Plaza de
España
Calle Santocildes
Calle de Hortelanos
Calle de San Juan
Arco de
San Juan
Río Vena
Calle de Santander
Calle del Cordón
Calle de la Puebla
Calle de San Lesmes
Casa del
Cordón
Plaza de
La Libertad
Calle de Vitoria
Calle de Toledo
Calle del Gran Teatro
Calle del Condestable
Avenida del Arlanzón
Plaza de
Mío Cid
Puente de San Pablo
Paseo de Sierra de Atapuerca
Plaza del
Conde de Castro
Correos

Page 119

Image of Nuestra Señora La Blanca. 17th century

You can tell you are in the medieval town by the presence of a number of singular elements, the ones disconnected from the others, which today have lost their urban and social functions but still possess a great historical and artistic value. This is the case of the walls and the castle, the parochial churches of San Esteban, San Nicolás, and San Gil, or the Santa Iglesia Catedral, and many of the treasures they contain. A specifically Burgos culture has exalted those times and identified the city with epic characters such as Fernán González or El Cid Campeador.

The route we would like to propose will lead you to the upper part of the castle's hill, from where you will be able to make out the secular process of urban development towards the river banks. You will reach the top of the hill from the west, skirting the wall, and cross the Puerta de San Martín and the Calle Tenebregosa, the main street in the Middle Ages, traversed by the Camino de Santiago and filled with monuments commemorating local heroes. From the castle you will climb down towards the quarters of San Esteban and San Gil, with their churches and their gates opened in the wall. Then you will descend eastwards in order to experience the entrepreneurial Burgos of the late Middle Ages, next to the river and the water channels, along several streets –San Juan Puebla, Comparada, Cantarranas la Mayor and la Menor: that is, today's Calle Santander, Calle la Moneda and Calle Almirante Bonifaz–, where the Constables of Castile erected their palace, the Casa del Cordón. Past the Plazas de los Mercados you will finally reach the cathedral, whose majestic profile marked the everyday life of the people of Burgos in that time.

Walls. Paseo de los Cubos

The **walls**. Walking west from the Arco de Santa María (2), up the Calle Eduardo Martínez del Campo, you will reach the Paseo de los Cubos and then the Puerta de San Martín, with the largest remaining stretch of wall.

The remains of the walls date from the 13th century. Their erection was promoted by the city council, under the auspices of Alfonso X. In 1276, the king congratulated the city for replacing a previous wall, of whose layout little is known, with a new one. In 1313 the works were still in progress. The walls went from the castle to the banks of the rivers Vena, Pico and Arlanzón.

There were different reasons to build the walls. There were, of course, military reasons, to ensure the defence of a city with a great political power, allied with the Crown and, consequently, the main target of military attacks by the nobility, often opposed to the king, as was the case during the Civil War that broke out in the mid 14th century, or during the War of Succession in the second half of the 15th century. There were also economic, legal and fiscal reasons. The walls physically separated the city, with its privileges and lawcodes, from the country and the surrounding villages, and were instrumental for the city to be able to control the municipal taxes. They even contributed to temporarily stopping the dispersion of the urban nucleus, concentrating most urban endeavours in the closed-in city. In reality, the walls were a necessary element for an important city like Burgos.

The **Puerta de la Judería**, located next to the Cubo de Doña Lambra, on the southern corner of the wall, was a minor gate used to access the Morería (Moorish) and Judería (Jewish) quarters.

The **Puerta de San Martín** was the exit point of the Camino de Santiago, after going through the city, and of the road to Valladolid and Palencia. It was also the entry point of the kings, who, before crossing it, swore an oath of allegiance to the lawcodes and privileges of the city. In the 16th century these upper quarters had deteriorated, and the Puerta de Santa María became the city's main entry point.

Past the Puerta de San Martín stand three of the monuments erected by the city to pay homage to renowned local heroes: the Solar del Cid (10), in the first place, and then the Solar del Empecinado and the Solar del Conde Fernán González (7). Past the diocesan seminary, on the left hand side, you will climb the castle hill.

The walls were erected with ashlar from Hontoria and Atapuerca –brick was applied in some parts– and were between eight and 10 metres high, with crenellations and turrets, square in the upper stretches and round in the lower ones.

The Puerta de San Martín was built in the 14th century by Moorish stonemasons. It is Mudéjar in style, with horseshoe arches and a mixture of stone and brick.

Walls and Puerta de San Martín, seen from the interior

The **Castillo** represents the very origins o the city. Originally, Burgos was a castle village built right next to the fortress (884), which was inhabited by the military. During the 10th century, it held out against the attacks o the Muslim armies. Later on, between the 11th and 13th centuries –the kingdom's border was then further south and the local population expanded down the hill towards the bank of the rive Arlanzón–, the castle was under the direct control of the Castilian monarchs and served as a gaol for high-rank pri-

Iglesia de San Esteban with the fortress in the background

soners and, occasionally, as a venue for diplomatic meetings and court celebrations.

Meanwhile, relations with the city became cooler. During the 14th century the castle changed hands several times. In the 15th century it was given to the Stúñiga family, who managed the fortress until the proclamation of the Catholic Monarchs. In those times there were frequent lawsuits and confrontations in the council, which led to the War of Succession, with the Stúñiga supporting Juana la Beltraneja and the city on the side of Isabel the Catholic. The castle surrendered in 1476, after an eight-month siege.

A few years later the castle was returned to the crown and used as a gunpowder factory and an artillery academy. By the late 16th cen-

The castle area contains a number of underground structures, such as wells, staircases and galleries. The well is almost seventy metres deep, and consists of a central cylinder, 1.78 metres in diameter, surrounded by a series of spindles, maybe six or seven, 1.4 metres in diameter, containing a 10-metre spiral staircase. Its purpose was to provide the inhabitants of the castle with water, mainly during sieges. It is made of ashlar, and dates probably from the 12th and 14th centuries. The underground galleries are more than twenty metres long and between six and ten metres deep, and run below the courtyard. The oldest ones were built in the 15th century during a siege. They are connected to the well and the staircase.

tury it had badly deteriorated, and not even the governors lived in it any longer. In 1736 the castle caught fire; it burned for several days, before the total indifference of the people of Burgos. The War of Independence awakened the ghosts of the past. The French reactivated the castle's military and strategic potential. Led by the general Dubreton, they barricaded themselves in the castle and were besieged by Lord Wellington. Finally, in 1813, when the castle was being abandoned by the French, it was blown up and totally destroyed.

Today the ruins of the castle are being restored, for its social and cultural recovery, with a natural park around it.

Interior of the Iglesia de San Esteban

The **Iglesia de San Esteban**, built in the Gothic style in the 14th century, is a beautiful structure, with polygonal apses featuring long windows and, at the lower end, a superb early 14th-century portal, a rose window and a tower, which was modified in the 15th century and in 1813, after the castle was blown up.

The church has three naves and polygonal chapels on the altar end, with cylindrical pillars accompanied by columns. It is an ample, clear space, which underwent restoration works during the late Gothic and Renaissance periods, by great masters such as Simón de Colonia, Nicolás de Vergara or Juan de Vallejo, who

Sepulchre of the Gumiel family

Iglesia de San Esteban

MUSEO DEL RETABLO

The Iglesia de San Esteban features a permanent exhibit of valuable altarpieces, paintings and silverwork from the different parishes of the Burgos diocese, mostly rural and dating from the 16th-18th centuries. Of particular interest are the altarpiece of the Virgen del Castrillo Matajudíos (16th century), the altarpiece representing the Last Supper in the same parish of San Esteban (16th-17th centuries) or the parochial chalice of Arroyo de Muño (15th century).

Altarpiece, Catrillo Matajudíos

Puerta de San Gil. City's escutcheon

built a series of notable tombs for the wealthy merchants' families, such as the Frías, Arceo or Gumiel families.

The **Puerta de San Esteban**, built, like the Puerta de San Martín, in the 14th century by Moorish stonemasons in the Mudéjar style, with horseshoe arches and a combination of brick and stone, is a unique monument, a faithful witness to the harmonious coexistence of different cultures.

The **Puerta de San Gil**, in its present form, dates from the 16th century. The arch is in the style of Juan de Vallejo and the upper building, rebuilt in 1557, was used

for different purposes by the council, for example as a gaol.

Attached to the old wall, today's Gothic **Iglesia de San Gil** was erected in the late 13th or early 14th century, on top of a previous Romanesque structure. The exterior plainness of the building is in contrast with the beauty and refinement of its interior. It has three naves, a transept and ribbed and star vaults; two 15th-century chapels flank the chancel.

The naves and chapels contain multiple manifestations of late Gothic and Renaissance art. The Capilla de la Natividad, the

Capilla de los Reyes, the Capilla de Nuestra Señora de la Buena Mañana and the Capilla de la Cruz are illustrative of the extremely refined technique and the educated sensitivity of the great Burgos masters who built the magnificent funereal monuments, at the service of wealthy merchant families such as the Castros, the Lermas, the Frías or the Sanvitores. The presbytery features a notable late 17th-century Baroque altarpiece, with a canvas painting of San Gil, by the artist Barranco.

Iglesia de San Gil. Capilla de la Natividad

Walking east, the wall disappears, due to the successive contemporary city expansion projects, and then you will reach the Puerta de San Juan.

The **Puerta de San Juan** is the easternmost city gate; an entry point for travellers, pilgrims and products from the north of the peninsula. It was virtually rebuilt in 1563, by the masters Simón de Bueras and Martín Ochoa de Arteaga. Two main streets, medieval in design but with a 19th-century look, begin here, the Calle de San Juan, which coincides with the Camino de Santiago (9) as it crosses the city, and the Calle de la Puebla, which leads directly to the Plaza del Mercado Mayor and to the Palace of the Constables of Castile, the so-called Casa del Cordón.

Iglesia de San Gil. Altarpiece of the Virgen de la Buena Mañana, by a member Gil de Siloe's school

The Iglesia de San Gil features the Capilla de la Natividad, a masterpiece following the style of the Capilla del Condestable: very high single-space octagonal structures, with a square ground plan, covered with ribbed vaults, resting on angular squinches. Work on the chapel started in 1529, as a funereal space for the Castro family.

Iglesia de San Gil. Capilla de la Natividad, detail.
Death of the Virgin. Felipe Vigarny's school

Iglesia de San Gil. Altarpiece of the Kings. Felipe Vigarny's school

The Casa del Cordón was a royal residence and the venue for great political and social events, as well as the urban home of the Velasco and Mendoza families. In it, for instance, the Catholic Monarchs received and lodged Christopher Columbus after his second voyage to America and, some years later, Gonzalo Fernández de Córdoba, the Great Captain; Felipe the Handsome and his wife the queen Juana also stayed here: the young king died in this house in September of 1506, after suddenly becoming sick at the age of 28, five months into his kingdom.

The **Casa del Cordón** is the most important manifestation of civil architecture before the 16th century. It was built by Simón de Colonia in the 1480's, at the request of the Constables of Castile Pedro Fernández de Velasco and his wife Mencía de Mendoza, with subsequent expansions in the 16th and 17th centuries. Particularly noteworthy is the portal facing the Mercado Mayor (Main Marketplace), which features a lintelled door and a Franciscan cord motif, giving the edifice its name, which frames different consoles with inscriptions allusive to the founders. In the 19th century the building underwent a series of radical transformations. In 1853 the two towers were rebuilt and in the following years new doors and windows were opened. The imposing balconies of the façade were built by Vicente Lampérez in the early 20th century. On the eastern side there is a gallery facing what once were the gardens of a typical 15th-century mansion. Inside there is a large yard. Recently the building was refurbished and turned into a branch of a financial institution known for its cultural sensitivity.

Since the Middle Ages, the southern square has always been the **Mercado Mayor** of the city. In the mid

9th century it was divided into two, when the block of houses known as the **Soportales de Antón** –after the hat shop by the same name– was erected, giving place to today's Plaza de la Libertad and Plaza de Santo Domingo de Guzmán.

Heading towards the Plaza Mayor you will see, to the right, a series of houses built during the expansion of the late Middle Ages: today's Calle de la Moneda, Calle del Almirante Bonifaz, and Calle de San Lorenzo.

At the **Calle de San Lorenzo** stands the **church** by the same name, built in the second half of the 17th century as the chapel of the Jesuit Colegio de El Salvador, under the auspices of Michaela de la Portilla, whose tomb can be seen in the presbytery. It has a Baroque front with columns, an image of the saint and different escutcheons. The main chapel has eight sides and is covered with barrel vaults with large windows and a dome resting on scallops. Particularly noteworthy is the rich decorative plasterwork covering most of the interior. When the Jesuits were expelled in 1767, the chapel was turned into a parochial church –the old Iglesia de San Llorente, in the Calle Tenebregosa, had been in ruins since the 16th century.

Iglesia de San Lorenzo

From the Calle de San Lorenzo, along the Calle de Laín Calvo, the former Calle de Trascorrales, which follows the course of a medieval water channel, and across the Arco del Pilar, you will reach the **Huerto del Rey**, next to the cathedral, also crossed by a water channel. In the 11th century it was the site of the palaces of Fernando I, hence the name, and, later on, of the houses of some of the wealthy bourgeois families of the 16th and 17th centuries.

The Calle de la Paloma, running parallel to one of the sides of the lower cloister of the cathedral, will take you back to the Plaza del Rey San Fernando (2) and the Arco de Santa María (2), your starting point.

Tower top, Iglesia de San Lorenzo

Huerto del Rey

In the centre of the Plaza del Huerto del Rey stands the Fuente de la Flora, a sample of the interest in urban decoration prevailing in the 18th century. Its main feature is a figure of the goddess Flora, by the Burgos artist Manuel Romero.

7 The Renaissance city

This route includes a visit to the southern suburbs, which, back in the 16th century, became the natural way of expansion of the medieval town and the site of palaces, funereal chapels and corporate edifices erected by private citizens and institutional bodies.

The Renaissance city

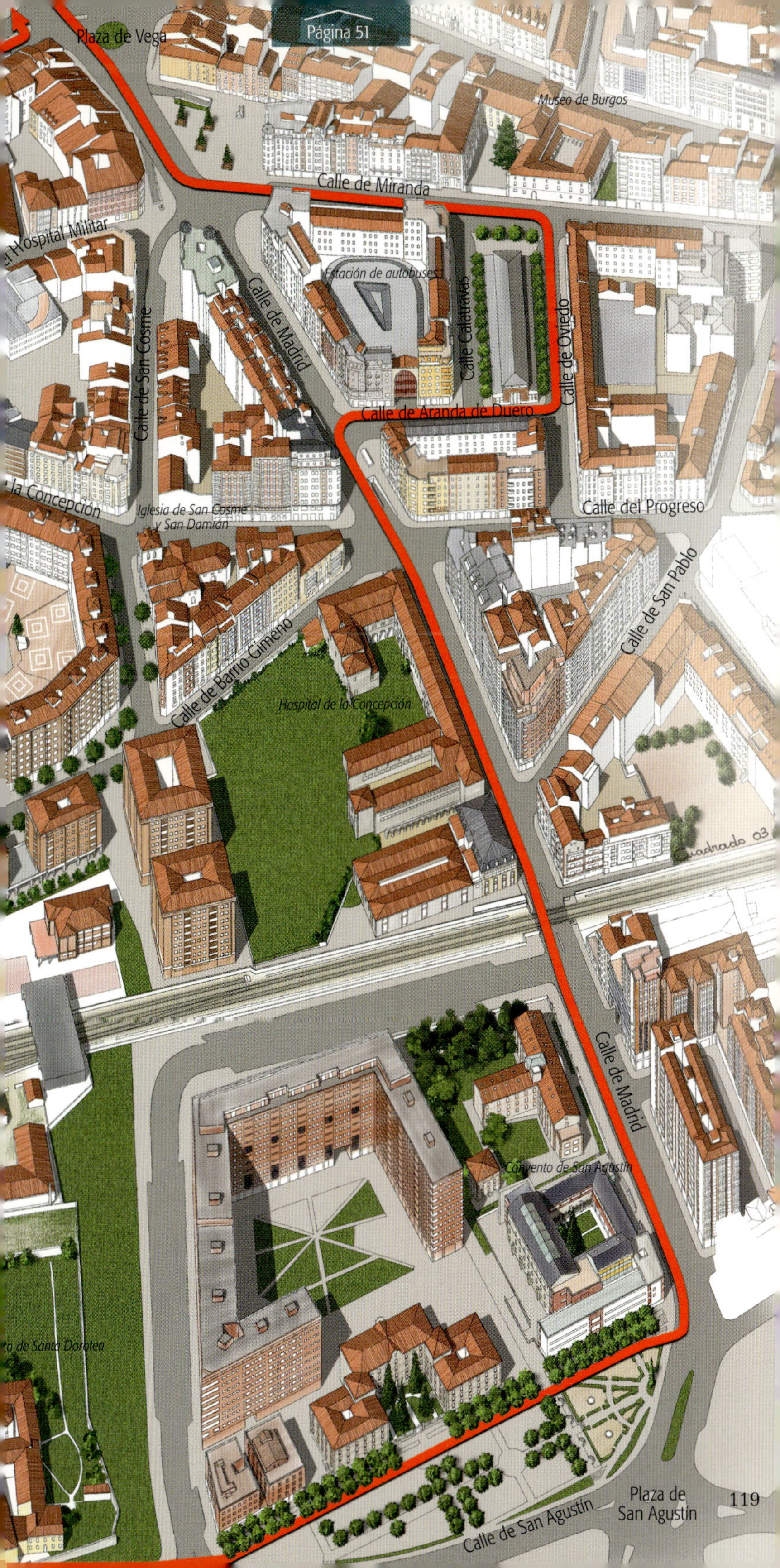

Página 51
Plaza de Vega
Museo de Burgos
Calle de Miranda
el Hospital Militar
Estación de autobuses
Calle Calatravas
Calle de Madrid
Calle de San Cosme
Calle de Oviedo
Calle de Aranda de Duero
Calle del Progreso
la Concepción
Iglesia de San Cosme
y San Damián
Calle de San Pablo
Calle de Barrio Gimeno
Hospital de la Concepción
Calle de Madrid
Convento de San Agustín
de Santa Dorotea
Plaza de
San Agustín
Calle de San Agustín

Loggia of the Casa de Miranda

Standing next to the Casa de Miranda, and dating from the same time, the Casa de Íñigo Angulo conserves its front and back façades and a three-sided patio. It was built at the request of Lope Hurtado de Mendoza, a knight of the Order of Saint James. It underwent important reforms in the 18th century, under the ownership of José B. Íñigo de Angulo.

Burgos became a consolidated city in the 16th century. Together with the successful trading and financial endeavours, the city developed an intense cultural activity, mainly due to the arrival in Burgos of Central European artists lured by the patronage of the wealthy local merchants.
The creative genius of Diego de Siloe, the refined technical skills of Felipe Vigarny, or the energetic expression of Simón de Bueras or García de Arredondo were forever imprinted in the city layout during this period, a true profusion of Renaissance works that gradually filled the streets, churches and palaces with a humane and realistic type of art.
Interesting samples of these works can be found in the southern suburbs of the city, along the following route.

Starting at the Arco de Santa María, across the bridge, by the Plaza de Vega, you will see the starting point of the Calle Calera, with several Renaissance works, such as the houses of Miranda and Íñigo Angulo, two unique samples of civil architecture, an optimum representation of Burgos humanism.

The **Casa de Miranda** was built in 1545, probably by Juan de Vallejo, as the residence of Francisco de Miranda. This exceptionally artistic building, with a Renaissance decoration, conserves the original main and rear fronts, the patio and the staircase, its most noble and harmonious parts. Today it houses the Museo de Burgos (4).

Casa de Iñigo Angulo

The **Hospital de la Concepción** is one of the most splendid 16th-century public edifices in the city. Its construction started in 1552, under the institutional auspices of the Brotherhood of the Conception and the patronage of the merchant Diego de Bernuy. Designed for the care of ill people, it was the first modern General Hospital in Burgos.

Hospital de la Concepción

The main front of the hospital's church is Renaissance in style and dates from the 17th century.

In 1779, members of the Enlightenment, determined to improve the educational system, created the Royal College of the School of Medicine and Surgery in the Hospital de la Concepción, later on transferred to the Convento de la Merced and finally closed in 1824.

Convento de San Agustín. Cloister

The **Convento de San Agustín**, run by the Canons Regular of the Rule of Saint Agustine, was a pilgrims' destination, since it was home to the image of the Holy Christ of Burgos until 1860, when it was brought to the cathedral. All that remains of the old convent is the remains of the cloister, built in the 13th century and reformed in the 15th. More recently it was superbly restored and turned into the offices of the cultural services of the Provincial Government.

Convento de Santa Dorotea. Bishop's sepulchre.

The **Convento de Santa Dorotea** was founded in the late 14th century by the lay sister Dorotea Rodríguez de Valderrama. It was established in its current location in 1470, with the patronage of Juan de Ortega, the first bishop of Almería.

The main late-Gothic church entrance is by Simón de Colonia, and features the coats of arms of the Catholic Monarchs and of the founder's family. It contains the sepulchre of the bishop, carved by Nicolás de Vergara in 1516, and of a relative of his, Alonso de Ortega, the main chaplain of the Infante Juan, the son of the Catholic Monarchs.

Iglesia de San Cosme y San Damián. Front

The **Iglesia de San Cosme y San Damián**, built for the most part in the early 16th century, features a beautiful Renaissance front by Juan de Vallejo, who was commissioned to build it in 1552. The tower dates from 1621. The church has three naves separated by pointed arches and lierne vaulting. The main altarpiece is Baroque and was built by Policarpo de la Nestosa in 1662, with sculptures by Juan de Pobes and Juan de los Helgueros. In the Gospel nave lies the sepulchre of the famous Renaissance screen maker Cristóbal de Andino and his wife Catalina de Frías.

Former Colegio de San Nicolás

The **Colegio de San Nicolás**, a high-school today, was originally conceived as a teaching centre thanks to the legacy of the cardinal Íñigo López de Mendoza. Most of the original structure, built between 1537 and 1579, has been preserved. Inside, the school has a central yard with arched galleries. The different premises orbit around this yard. The façade combines the Gothic elements of the buttresses and windows of the lower level with the Mannerism of the superb portal by the sculptor Diego Guillén.

Iglesia de la Merced. The Order of Mercy settled in Burgos around 1272, next to the Hospital de San Lázaro. In 1419 it moved to its current location, with the patronage of the Cartagena family. The late-Gothic church was built in the late 15th and the early 16th centuries, under the auspices of Francisco del Castillo and his wife Leonor Pesquera, who lie buried in the presbytery.

Iglesia de la Merced

Casa de los Cubos, the site of a soon-to-be-built pilgrims' hostel

In addition to the above, other Renaissance structures were erected along the main street within the walls, the one used by the Camino de Santiago, such as the **Casa de los Cubos**, named after the two cubes resting on scallops on both sides of the front; the **Casa de los Lerma**, next to the previous one, which conserves the front wall of the lower floor; or the **Palacio de Castilfalé**, located opposite the Puerta de la Coronería of the cathedral, built by Juan de Vallejo, at the request of the wealthy merchant Nicolás de Gauna in the mid 16th century. It has undergone many transformations; the lower level of the main front, the hall, the staircase and the patio are the oldest parts of the house. Today it holds the Municipal Archives.

Palacio de Castilfalé. Front

On the same street, further up in the direction of the Puerta de San Martín (6), you will find the **Arco de Fernán González**, a triumphal monument of 1580,

Arco de Fernán González

erected by the city to pay homage to the first count of Castile. It is a plain, classicist structure by Juan de Ortega de Castañeda, shaped as a pointed arch flanked by columns and topped by several escutcheons, with a dedication signed by Fray Luis de León. And the **Alhóndiga**, the city's cereal repository, which conserves the main front and other exterior parts, with early Renaissance elements in the style of Francisco de Colonia. The interior has undergone deep modifications, first to be adapted as a provincial jail and, more recently, as a cultural centre.

Outside the route described, there are other Renaissance works in the following locations:
a) Convento de Santa Clara. Built under the pope Gregory IX in 1232. The Salamanca and Polanco patrician families financed the enlargement and restoration works during the 15th century. The church dates from the second half of the 13th century, with some additions of the 13th. It has some Baroque altarpieces.
b) Convento de las Bernardas. Founded in the 16th century in the houses of Andrés de Melgosa, which preserved the stone fronts and the patio. Today it holds the conservatorium.

Convento de las Bernardas. Front

La Alhóndiga

8 The bourgeois city

The old quarter of Burgos as we know it today was created by the members of the Enlightenment and the liberal bourgeoisie of the 19th century. The medieval town was deeply transformed after the implementation by the new bourgeois classes of new, more comfortable and beautiful urban concepts.

DE RECREO

The bourgeois city

Iglesia de San Gil
Palacio de Capitanía
Plaza de Alonso Martínez
C/ de la Concordia
Avenida del Cid Campeador
C/ Santocildes
Calle de Avellanos
Calle de San Juan
Arco del Pilar
Iglesia de San Lorenzo
Calle de San Lorenzo
Calle del Almirante Bonifaz
Calle de la Moneda
Calle de Santander
Plaza del Huerto del Rey
Calle de Laín Calvo
Casa del Cordón
Plaza de Sto. Domingo
Plaza de la Libertad
Calle de Vitoria
Plaza Mayor
Palacio de la Diputación
Ayuntamiento
Teatro Principal
Plaza de Mío Cid
Consulado del Mar
Paseo del Espolón
Paseo de Marceliano Santa María
Puente de San Pablo
Plaza del Conde de Castro
Calle de Valladolid
Plaza de Vega
Museo de Burgos
Calle de Miranda
Calle de Madrid
Calle de San Pablo

Calle de Laín Calvo. Balconies

Calle de Laín Calvo. Detail

Paseo del Espolón. Detail

The historic centre of Burgos, as we see it today, was basically built by the Enlightenment and the liberal bourgeoisie of the 19th century. The medieval city was deeply transformed by the illustrated classes, with a new, more comfortable and beautiful notion of the urban space.

The old water channels were covered up or diverted, the bridges disappeared and the streets were extended with perfectly lined-up rows of houses featuring uniform, classical, elegant fronts representing the tastes and customs of the new times.

The river Alanzón became a part of the city, its course turned into an urban axis. Its waters were channelled by a solid ashlars wall, and spacious promenades were built on its banks. These promenades were soon to become the new city's showcase, a place to see and be seen, oblivious of the nearby medieval enclosure. Gradually, new public buildings were built in order to take care of the new local and provincial administrative functions –such as the Casa Consistorial and the Casa del Consulado, the Diputación Provincial or the Audiencia Territorial–, the military services –such as Capitanía or the Hospital Militar–, or the city's social assistance and recreational services –such as the Casa de Beneficencia, in land plots of San Agustín, and the Teatro Principal, at one end of the Paseo del Espolón. On its part, the Church contributed to the city's development by building a series of outstanding edifices, such as the Palacio Arzobispal, the Seminario de San Jerónimo or the Iglesia de las Salesas.

New structures were also added to this modern, bourgeois, liberal city during the first half of the 20th century, in the southern extension of the city, between the Calle de Miranda and the Calle de Madrid, in the prolongation of the Calle de Vitoria and in a number of popular quarters. Inexpensive housing was built in a number of popular quarters, for the working people living in the urban periphery.

A good place to start the tour is the Calle de la Paloma, next to the cathedral, which will lead you along the Calle de Laín Calvo, with its typically bourgeois houses and balconies, up to Capitanía General.

The **Palacio de Capitanía General** was designed in 1903 by the Burgos architect Saturnino Martínez Ruiz, to replace the old Palacio de las Cuatro Torres. It is a finished example of the historicist building trend that took inspiration from the old medieval styles.

Palacio de Capitanía

On its part, the **Palacio de la Diputación Provincial**, built between 1864 and 1869, in the Isabelline period, on the site of the gaol, was designed by the architects Luis Villanueva and Ángel Calleja, both renowned for their solid academic training. It is a monumental structure in the classical tradition, with palatial reminiscences. It contains samples of the work of some Burgos artists.

Palacio de la Diputación Provincial

The adjacent **Teatro Principal**, also Classical in style, was built between 1843 and 1858, next to the Paseo del Espolón, in an area that used to be in the course of the river Arlanzón. Its designer, Francisco Angoitia, developed a project emulating the style of the theatres of the 19th century, with a rectangular ground plan, a large central area and stage, surrounded by multi-purpose premises. The exterior of the building features Italian elements and a refined decoration. A new structure was added in 1884, facing the Paseo del Espolón, commonly known as El Polisón. The complex has been recently restored, and has recovered its original use.

Teatro Principal

Along the Paseo del Espolón (7), the largest contribution of the bourgeoisie to the civic structure of the city, as indicated above, and

The Red Room

Teatro Principal. Boxes

past the back of the Casa Consistorial (2), you will reach the **Casa del Consulado**. It was built in 1795, at the request of the Consulado del Mar, in order to house a modern Drawing School, in line with the precepts of the

North of the Teatro Principal, facing the Palacio de la Diputación, is the Morito, a charming clock that has marked the passage of time for Burgos citizens since 1860.

Enlightenment, which promoted artistic education. It was designed by Manuel de Eraso in a sober, Classical style, and is topped with a pediment and an anchor, the symbol of the consular institution.

Another group of outstanding monuments of the 19th and early 20th centuries can be seen in the westernmost sector of the Paseo del Espolón, along the Paseo de la Isla, and to the right of the Arco de Santa María, including:

The **Seminario de San Jerónimo**, a structure dating from the second half of the 19th century, built as an extension of the old seminary of the Calle de Nuño Rasura, in order to lodge a growing community of seminarists. It is a surprisingly plain and monotonous structure, except for the portals of the side and central sections.

The **Palacio Arzobispal**, by Javier de Luque and Julián Apráiz, takes inspiration from the eclecticism of the 19th century, combining different historical styles, with the predominance of the Renaissance and the Baroque periods. Topping the main front is an Episcopal shield, medallions featuring the four evangelists, the escutcheon of Burgos, the Marian jar of lilies and the date of construction (1916).

Seminario de San Jerónimo

Palacio Arzobispal

The **Palacio de Justicia**. The last third of the 19th century saw the harmonious convergence of the traditional, Classical architecture, respectful with the academic norms, and other building languages. The Palacio de Justicia is in line with this

Palacio de Justicia

Classical tradition, which searches simplicity within a great formal solemnity. Built in 1874 by the architect David Ruiz Jareño, it harmoniously combines a neo-Hellenistic style with the landscaped gardens of the Paseo de la Isla (11).

The **Iglesia de las Salesas**. The architectural eclecticism of the late 19th and early 20th centuries left some outstanding monuments in the city, incorporating the neo-Gothic forms, with a long tradition in the history of Burgos art. This can be seen in the Iglesia de la Salesa, by the architect Juan M. Lázaro, and in the nearby Convento de las Hijas de Jesús, by Vicente Lampérez.

Gate, Paseo de la Isla. Medallion

Gate, Paseo de la Isla. Detail

Iglesia de las Salesas

9 Camino de Santiago

Burgos and the Camino de Santiago would not be what they are today without each other. Actually, they came into being and grew up together, quietly influencing each other, particularly during the Middle Ages, between the 11th and 15th centuries, the heyday of pilgrimages. Pilgrims were a breath of fresh air in Europe, bringing along a new culture and the same faith which, in combination with the local culture, resulted in the cultural crossbreeding on which today's European unity is based.

Camino de Santiago

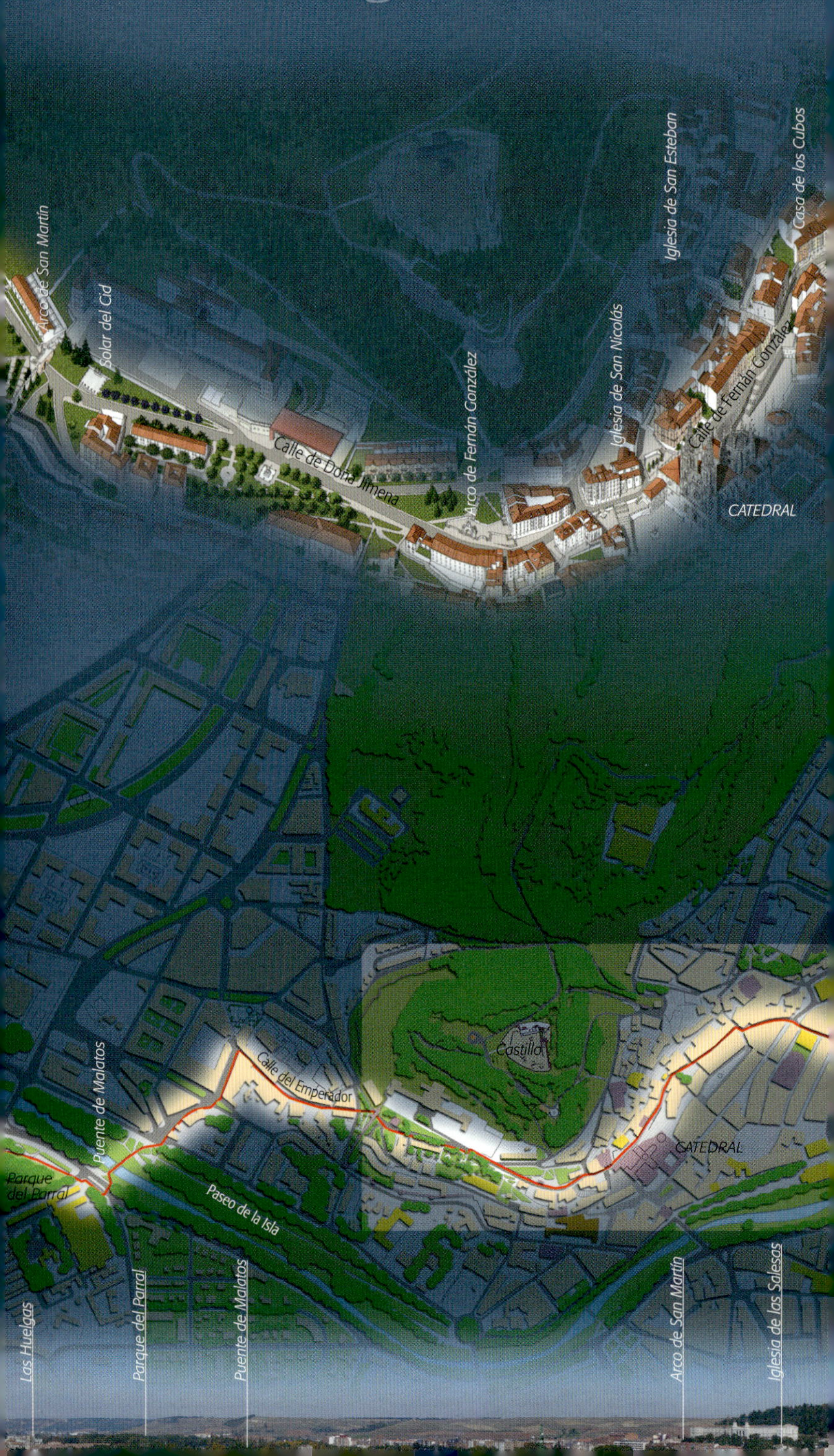

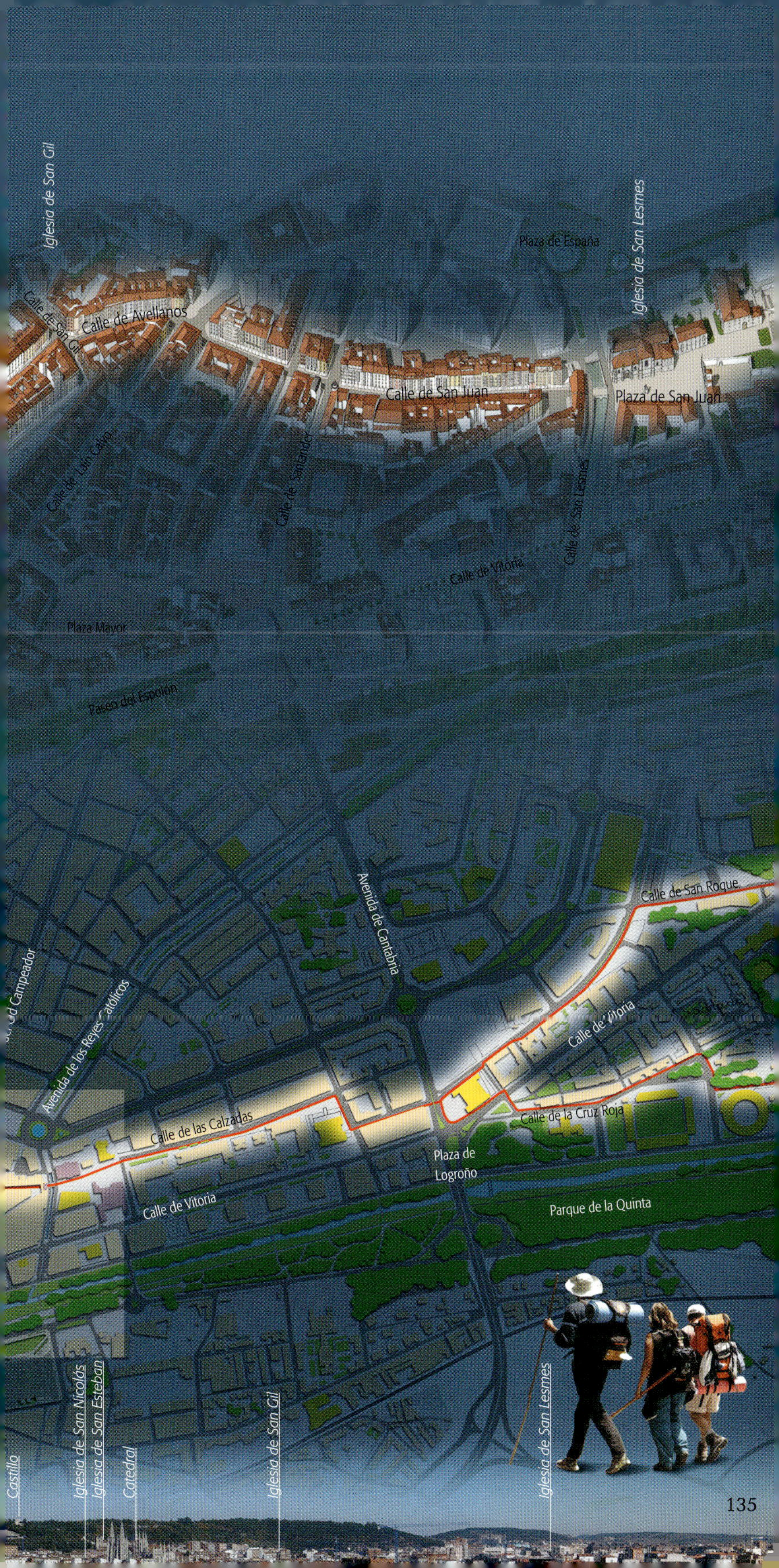
Iglesia de San Gil
Plaza de España
Iglesia de San Lesmes
Calle de San Gil
Calle de Avellanos
Calle de San Juan
Plaza de San Juan
Calle de Laín Calvo
Calle de Santander
Calle de San Lesmes
Calle de Vitoria
Plaza Mayor
Paseo del Espolón
Avenida de Cantabria
Calle de San Roque
Campeador
Avenida de los Reyes
Calle de Vitoria
Calle de las Calzadas
Calle de la Cruz Roja
Plaza de Logroño
Calle de Vitoria
Parque de la Quinta
Castillo
Iglesia de San Nicolás
Iglesia de San Esteban
Catedral
Iglesia de San Gil
Iglesia de San Lesmes

In the heyday of pilgrimages, between the 11th and 15th centuries, pilgrims were a breath of fresh European air, bringing along a new culture and faith, which, in combination with the local traditions, resulted in the cultural mixture that lies beneath the European unity.

Pilgrims left their mark in Burgos, along the longitudinal line of its layout, and many of them, the so-called francos, stayed here for good, promoting the city's commercial activity and craft industry.

In the meantime, the city provided its dwellers with a level of material and spiritual assistance unmatched by any other city in those times.

Gothic Calvary, Iglesia de Gamonal

From Gamonal to Burgos along the Calzadas

Pilgrims reached Burgos after visiting the Marian sanctuary of **Nuestra Señora la Real y Antigua** in Gamonal. The church that you see today dates from the 14th century. It has a Latin cross ground plan, one nave, a transept and a quadrangular chapel. It also has a powerful tower, with a masonry portico, built later on. Inside there is a Calvary, featuring wooden figures of great expressive power, dating from the late 13th or early 14th century, and the image of the Virgin and Child, from the second half of the 13th century. Next to the portico stands the 15th-century transept, related with the Camino de Santiago, with a representation of Christ Crucified and the Virgin accompanied by Saint James Pilgrim, among other biblical characters.

Nuestra Señora La Real y Antigua de Gamonal

The Camino de Santiago goes on along the Calle de las Calzadas –a plural term, due to the convergence at that point of the Gamonal and Capiscol calzadas (roads)– and then it reaches the Puerta de San Juan. Before crossing this gate, pilgrims could use the services offered in the complex –consisting of a monastery, a hospital and a church– erected by Saint Lesmes, a French Benedictine monk, in the late 11th century.

The Renaissance cloister and chapter room, and the **Museum**, dedicated to the Burgos Artist **Marceliano Santamaría**, are all that remains of the **Monasterio de San Juan**.

Of the original **Hospital de San Juan** there are only a few remnants in the front and the coats of arms by Simón de Colonia, in today's Casa de la Cultura. They come from the hospital that was founded in 1476, dedicated to Saint John the Baptist, at the initiative of the monks, the city council and the Universidad de Mercaderes. The original hospital was donated by Alfonso I to Saint Lesmes in 1091.

The **Iglesia de San Lesmes** contains the mortal remains of Saint Lesmes, the city's patron saint since 1511. In the 13th century the church was separated from the monastery and the hospital. Today's structure was erected at different stages during the 15th and 16th centuries. It has a late Gothic front by the Colonia workshop. The belfry dates from 1665. The church has three naves, with three sec-

Gamonal transept

Saint James as a pilgrim. Gamonal's transept

Burgos was the first large city pilgrims saw alter crossing the Pyrenees. At that time (15th century) Burgos was densely populated, it had political weight, beautiful monuments and all the things necessary for the way. And, above all, it had a solid, both public and private, assistance infrastructure, including a cathedral, fifteen parochial churches, several monasteries and more than thirty hospitals for pilgrims.

Former Hospital de San Juan

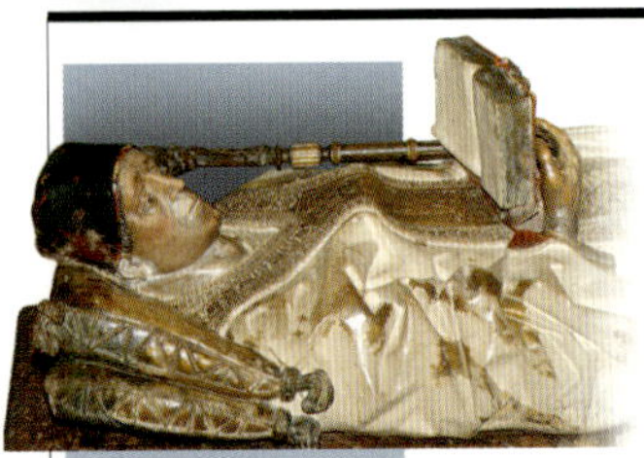

At the foot of the presbytery of the Iglesia de San Lesmes is the sepulchre of the patron Saint, a highly realistic stone effigy dating from the 15th century, by the Master of Covarrubias.

tions each, and a transept, a polygonal altar end and ribbed vaulting, and contains outstanding works of art dating from between the late Gothic and Baroque periods. Particularly noteworthy is the altarpiece of the Capilla de los Salamanca, which illustrates the popularity of the large funereal monuments in the late 15th century, or the 1533 Renaissance pulpit by the master Juan de Salas. The main unpainted altarpiece is Baroque and dates from the mid 18th century.

In the centre of the square stands a statue dedicated to the founder of the city, the count Diego Porcelos, by Juan de Avalos (1984).

Iglesia de San Lesmes, front

Flemish altarpiece. Capilla de los Salamanca. Iglesia de San Lesmes

Along the calle de San Juan, up to the Puerta de San Martín

Past the Puerta de San Juan you will reach the street by the same name, a medieval, fully Jacobean

Iglesia de San Lesmes

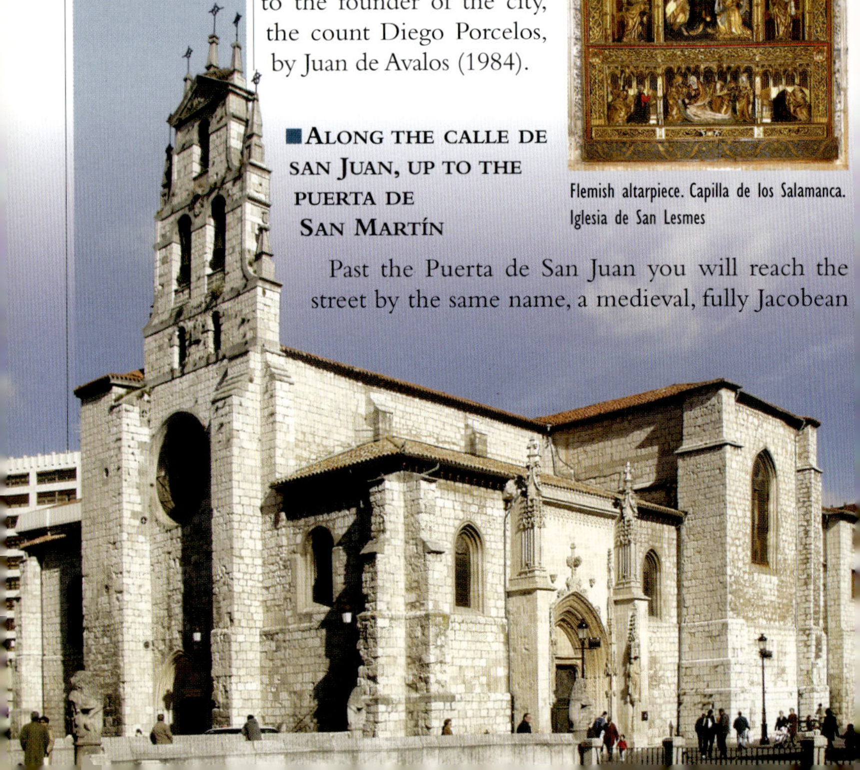

Plaza de San Juan

Calle de San Juan

street, gentrified by the bourgeoisie after the reforms undertaken in the 19th century. The buildings are compact, with similar heights and façades covered with refined ornaments, cornices and moulds. They feature the typical covered balconies, to provide protection from the cold and ensure the comfortable contemplation of street life, within the framework of a new culture of leisure.

Up the Calle Avellanos, crossing the Calle de San Gil and along the consecutive Calles de San Llorente, Coronería, Tenebregosa and Viejarrúa –today's Calle de Fernán González–, you will reach the Puerta de San Martín (6), at the other end of the city. In total, around 1,350 metres door to door, which allowed pilgrims to visit, without veering off their route, the cathedral, accessed directly via the Puerta de la Coronería, the Iglesia de San Nicolás and the long-gone churches of San Llorente, Santiago, San Román, Nuestra Señora de la Vieja Rúa and San Martín, plus a plethora of private inns and small hostels and hospitals, whose doors were always open to the poor, the pilgrims and the sick. In their lieu, today you will find the Casa de los Cubos (7), the Casa de los Lerma (7), the Palacio de Castilfalé (7), the Arco de Fernán González (7), the statue of El Empecinado and the Solar del Cid, before finally reaching the Puerta de San Martín (6). That used to be the city's exit point, for those headed towards the quarter of San Pedro, where once stood the Hospital del Emperador. The Puente del los Malatos led pilgrims towards the Hospital del Rey.

Escutcheons of Castile and Burgos, Puente de San Juan

■ THE HOSPITAL DEL REY, A MODEL FOR OTHER LARGE HOSPITALS

Founded around 1200 by Alfonso VIII and his wife Leonor of Aquitaine, no other medieval hospital had bet-

Puente de los Malatos

ter facilities in the Camino de Santiago. It was run by a community of 12 lay brethren and 12 lay sisters of the Cistercian rule, led by the abbess of the Monasterio de las Huelgas, and had among its patrons the monarchs of Castile, who granted it exceptional rents and privileges. Today it is the site of the Rectorate and the Law School of the University of Burgos.

The Hospital del Rey in figures. In order to have an idea of its economy and the services provided, let's take a look at the following information, dating back to 1499. It had 87 beds, 66 for men an 21 for women, 45 of them in dormitories and 42 in infirmaries, and provided meals, on a daily basis, to an average of 200 pilgrims and sick or poor people. The pilgrim's menu consisted of 575 grams of white bread, a litre of wine, a bowl of vegetable soup and a piece of ram meat weighing around 300 grams. Except for the sick people, no one could stay more than one night. Its annual income was around 1,600,000 maravedis, 7,000 fanegas of wheat an

Patio de los Romeros

barley, 300 fanegas of salt and 2,500 heads of seasonal migrating sheep, plus 1,500 rams and 1,000 sheep to be selected every year from other ranchers' cattle during the crossing of the Madrid mountain range, a special privilege reserved to the Crown.

Some elements of the 13th century have been preserved, such as the two pre-Gothic fronts leading into the church or the bare pillars of the old church-hospital, and some interesting 16th-century works, such as the Patio de Romeros, with a door and portico of the same name, one of the most beautiful and better preserved architectural groups of the Spanish Renaissance, featuring a rich Jacobean iconography. A series of subsequent expansions gave place to new, spacious infirmaries.

Hospital del Rey

As opposed to this hospital model, there was also small urban hospitals, established in family residences, with small rents administered by a parish or brotherhood, which offered pilgrims little more than a roof to protect themselves from the weather, a fire and, maybe, one of the very few –usually four or six– beds available to spend the night.

Hospital del Rey. Church door. Juan de Valmaseda's school. First third of the 16th century

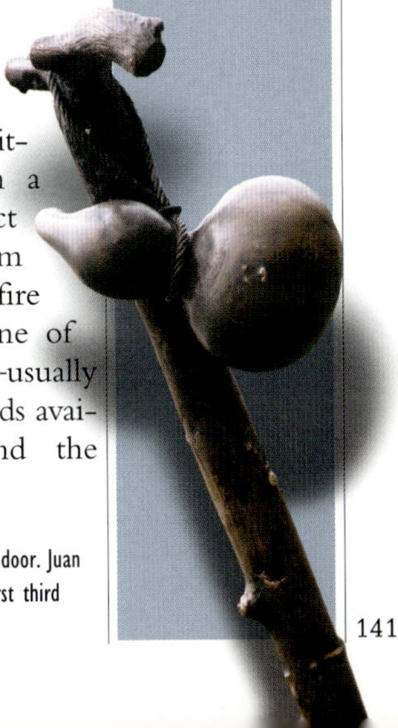

10

Ruta de El Cid

Together with the cathedral, the other historical icon supporting Burgos' claim to international fame is Rodrigo Díaz, El Cid Campeador. His passionate personality nurtured a number of myths and legends, in which Burgos was inextricably involved.

Ruta de El Cid

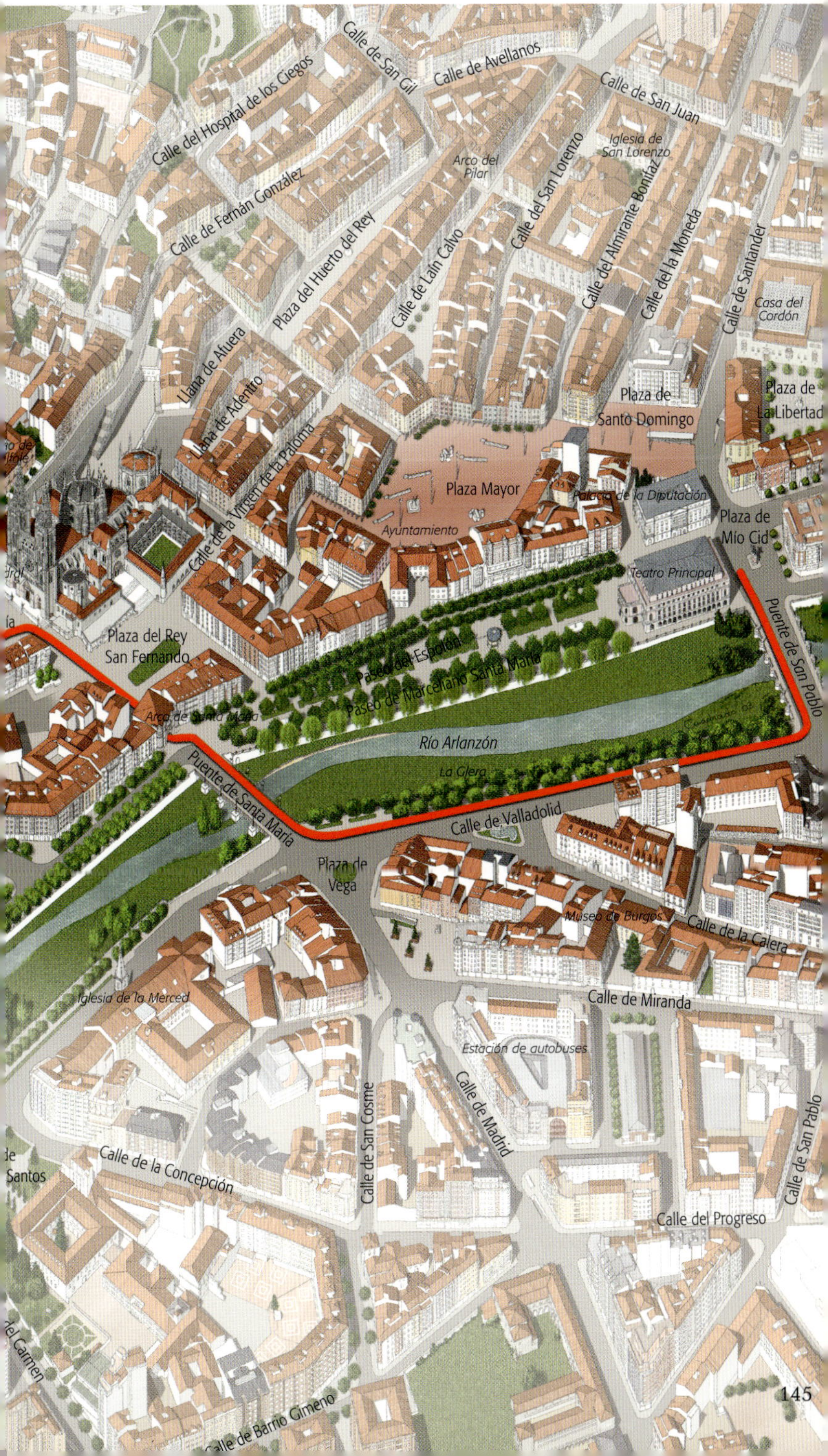
Calle de San Gil
Calle de Avellanos
Calle de San Juan
Calle del Hospital de los Ciegos
Iglesia de San Lorenzo
Arco del Pilar
Calle de Fernán González
Calle del San Lorenzo
Calle del Almirante Bonifaz
Calle de la Moneda
Calle de Santander
Casa del Cordón
Plaza del Huerto del Rey
Calle de Laín Calvo
Llana de Afuera
Llana de Adentro
Plaza de Santo Domingo
Plaza de La Libertad
Calle de la Vírgen de la Paloma
Plaza Mayor
Palacio de la Diputación
Ayuntamiento
Plaza de Mío Cid
Teatro Principal
Plaza del Rey San Fernando
Paseo del Espolón
Paseo de Marceliano Santa María
Puente de San Pablo
Arco de Santa María
Río Arlanzón
La Glera
Puente de Santa María
Calle de Valladolid
Plaza de Vega
Museo de Burgos
Calle de la Calera
Iglesia de la Merced
Calle de Miranda
Estación de autobuses
Calle de Madrid
Calle de San Cosme
Calle de San Pablo
Calle de la Concepción
Santos
Calle del Progreso
Calle de Barrio Gimeno

El Cid Campeador, a universal Burgos character, was born in Vivar, 10 km north of the city. According to the author of thePoema del mío Cid (Poem of El Cid), he had a close relationship with the City by the Arlanzón. And this relationship became even closer when he was turned into a literary character and a myth, forever identified with Burgos.

"Castile is becoming wider" by Marceliano Santa María, City Hall

HISTORICAL EL CID

Rodrigo Diaz was born around 1048 into a family of the Castilian nobility, with good connections with the king of Castile and León, Fernando I, which granted him, during the earlier years of his life, the friendship of the crown's heir, the future king Sancho II of Castile. Upon his death during the siege of Zamora, the king was succeeded by his brother Alfonso VI, with whom our hero was to renovate his oaths of loyalty and friendship. A consequence of this would be his marriage to Jimena, the king's cou-

Sculpture by Diego Rodríguez, Puente de San Pablo

Old sepulchre of El Cid, Monasterio de Cardeña

sin, in 1704, as well as the royal concession of protection privileges over his estate and noble rights in 1705, or his travelling to Andalusia in 1079 as the personal representative of the king in order to collect the taxes that the Moorish kings of Córdoba and Seville owed to the Castilian monarch.

This friendship, however, came to a sudden end in 1081, when El Cid decided to intervene with his private army, without the authorization of the king, in the Muslim lands of Toledo, which brought about the king's wrath and the first banishment of El Cid from the Castilian territory.

From then onwards, the life of El Campeador (The Champion) changed radically. Until then he had divided his time into living at home, enjoying the luxuries of the Court, managing his domains, and fulfilling his duties to the Crown, as corresponded to a noble subject of the king. From that moment onwards, however, he became a soldier of fortune.

He soon offered his services to the count of Barcelona, but was rejected, and, later on, to the Moorish king of Zaragoza, who welcomed him with open arms. From 1081 to 1087, El Cid followed the orders of his new protector, collaborating effectively in the defence of his interests.

In 1087 he returned to Toledo to participate, on the side of Alfonso VI, in the defence of the Castilian kingdom, which was then seriously endangered by the at-

Sculpture of Ben Galbón, Puente de San Pablo

Sculpture of San Sisebuto, Puente de San Pablo

The first feat of El Cid by Evaristo Barrio, City Hall

The Oath of Santa Gadea by Andrés García Prieto, Diputación Provincial

tacks of the Almoravids. When mutual trust was restored, the king of Castile and León commissioned him to pacify the eastern territories and collect the taxes due.

But a new unfortunate confrontation with the king, at the end of 1089, would lead to his second banishment, much harder than the first one, since it included the confiscation of all his property. From then on, he focussed on the practice of war even more intensely, acting on an individual basis, without being subjected to any acknowledged authority.

He travelled back to the Mediterranean, where he enjoyed a period of military success due to his diplomatic and strategic skills. In 1902 he subjected the city of Valencia under the supreme authority of the Crown of Castile, and he did it again two years later. El Cid became the lord of Valencia and the surrounding territory, successfully defending it from the attacks of the Almoravids. After his death, in 1099, Valencia was again taken by the Muslims. In 1101, the king Alfonso VI evacuated the city and granted life-long safety and sustenance to the widow of El Cid.

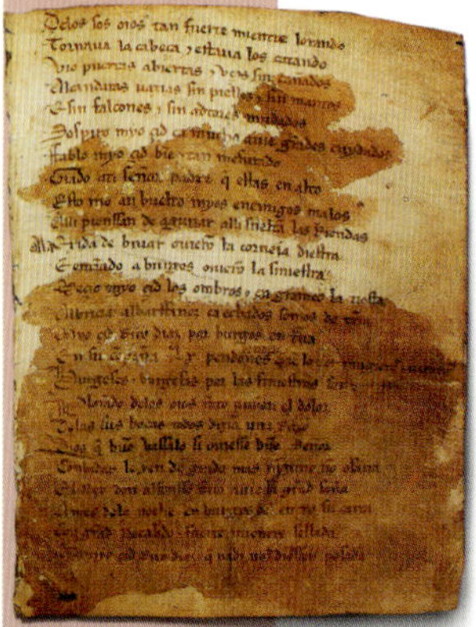

The Poem of El Cid

■ Legendary El Cid

A series of episodes were attributed to the legendary El Cid over the years, in an attempt to enhance his human, warring, patriotic and Christian values.

This is the case, for instance, with some details concerning his banishment, the wedding of his daughters or the Affront of Corpes, as described in the *Poem of El Cid* (circa 1200-1210), the Oath of Santa Gadea, narrated by Lucas de Tuy in his *Chronicon Mundi* of 1236, or the death of Rodrigo in odour of sanctity as described in the *First General Chronicle*, written around 1280-1290. The 15th-century *Mocedades de Rodrigo* deals with the exploits performed during his adolescent years. After the Middle Ages, the myth overshadowed both the literary character and the man, particularly in Burgos. That explains the monument built by the city council in his honour (1784), the solemn removal of his mortal remains to the cathedral (1921), or Franco's inauguration of the equestrian statue next to the Puente de San Pablo (1955).

The following route will help you to identify the main episodes and places that have been preserved in connection with El Campeador.

Iglesia de Santa Agueda

According to the oral tradition collected in the Chronicles and in the Spanish ballads, it was here that El Cid made Alfonso VI swear he had not been involved in the murder of his brother Sancho; the king, angered by El Cid's mistrust, banished him from Castile. There is a plaque commemorating this event.

Oath plaque

The 15th-century Gothic Iglesia de Santa Águeda was erected on the site of a former Romanesque structure. It has a single nave with four sections covered with vaults dating from the 16th century. The pilasters of the nave are what remains of the original Romanesque building. There are some elaborate burial monuments featuring Renaissance motifs. The Neo-Gothic main altarpiece, of alabaster, was built in the mid-20th century by the Burgos sculptor Sotillos.

Solar del Cid

Solar del Cid

According to tradition, this used to be the site of the urban residence of El Cid Campeador, by the Camino de Santiago. In 1593 the Burgos council had plans to erect a commemorating monument in some houses that the monks of the Monasterio de Cardeña owned in Burgos, known as the Casas del Cid Ruí Díaz. The monument that you can see today, dating from 1784, was built by José Cortés; on a pedestal stand the escutcheons of Burgos and San Pedro de Cardeña, and, in the middle, a commemorative plaque containing the coat of arms of El Cid, by Manuel Campillo.

Tizona

The tomb of El Cid and Jimena

The mortal remains of El Cid and of his wife Jimena lie buried under the spectacular transept of the cathedral since 1921. Before that, they had rested in the Monasterio de San Pedro de Cardeña (11). During the French occupation they were kept in the Espolón, and in 1842 they were transferred to the chapel of the Casa Consistorial, until they were definitely removed to their current location.

Tomb of El Cid and Jimena

Cofre de El Cid

Kept in a wall of the Capilla del Corpus Christi (1), tradition has it this was the chest, supposedly full of coins but actually full of sand, with which El Cid intended to maintain his armed retinue, given to him by the Jews Rachel and Vidas as he left Burgos into exile.

■ Arco de Santa María (2)

Figures of the Poem of El Cid, by Marceliano Santa María, Arco de Santa María

In the exterior front, El Cid forms part of the series of heroes and saints accompanying Charles I. It contains a bone, with a certificate of authenticity, a replica of the sword Tizona, taken by El Campeador from the king Bucar of Morocco, and a painting by the Burgos artist Marceliano Santamaría representing El Cid and Jimena.

■ La glera

La Glera

La Glera, a gravelly area next to the river and near the Puerta de Santa María, is where El Cid and his cohort set up camp during the first night of his exile, since, according to the poem, the king had prohibited the people of Burgos to put him up in their houses. A monolith commemorates this event, with a few passionate verses.

■ Puente de San Pablo

The bridge over the river Arlanzón is flanked by a series of stone statues representing characters related with the figure of El Cid. These sculptures, the result of a competition organised by the Burgos City Hall in 1953, are by Joaquín Lucarini, a Bilbao sculptor with an Italian background. The eight statues, spatially and thematically connected to the equestrian statue of El Cid, seem to accompany the hero as he rides into exile.

■ Equestrian statue

This monumental work was sculpted in bronze by Juan Cristóbal, with the collaboration of the architect Fernando Chueca Goitia, and inaugurated with great solemnity in 1955. Holding the sword in the air, his cape blowing in the wind, wearing a long beard and standing on the stirrups, El Cid arrogantly rides into exile.

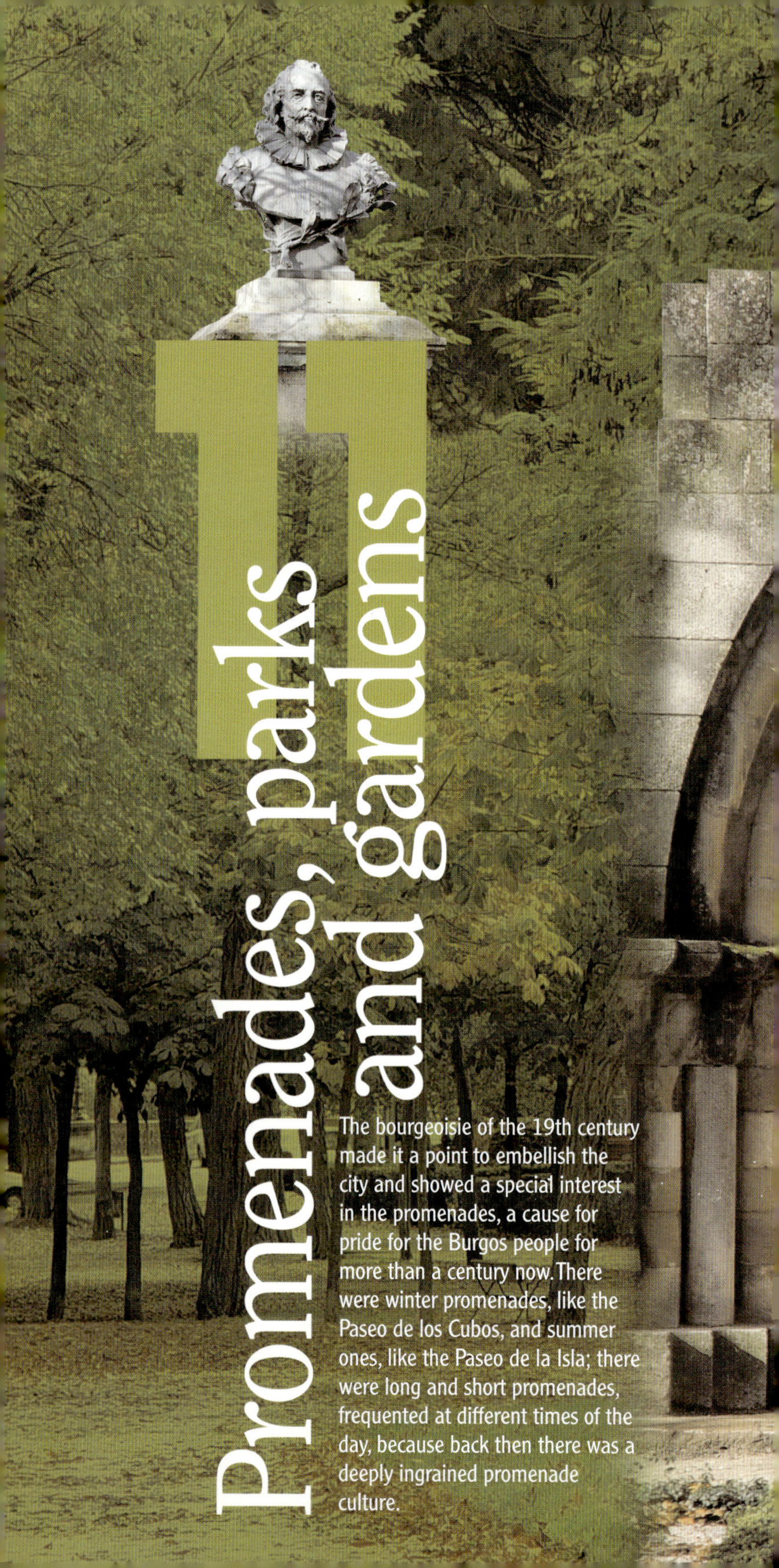

11 Promenades, parks and gardens

The bourgeoisie of the 19th century made it a point to embellish the city and showed a special interest in the promenades, a cause for pride for the Burgos people for more than a century now. There were winter promenades, like the Paseo de los Cubos, and summer ones, like the Paseo de la Isla; there were long and short promenades, frequented at different times of the day, because back then there was a deeply ingrained promenade culture.

There are several kilometres of parks and promenades, which allow visitors to cross the city from east to west under the shade of the trees. The river Arlanzón, a genuinely Castilian river, dry, bony, silent –one feels like offering it a glass of water, as Emilio Bobadilla once said– marks the way.

Paseo del Espolón. Gardens

The most emblematic of the city's promenades is, as indicated above, the **Paseo del Espolón** (2), an old path skirting the wall, between the Puerta de San Pablo and the Puerta de Santa María, turned by the Enlightenment into a natural promenade and, since then, into the main artery of the city.

In its southern prolongation, between the Arco de Santamaría and the Plaza de Castilla, the Espolón becomes the **Paseo de la Isla**. This is an exclusively bourgeois space, featuring a number of public buildings erected during the last third of the 19th century, such as the old Banco de España, designed by Eduardo de Adaro, or the Colegio de las Hijas del Niño Jesús, all of them featuring an interesting combination of red brick and Hontoria stone. At the end of the promenade, the Plaza de Castilla is adorned with a beautiful jar by the local artist Fortunato Julián.

Plaza de Castilla. Vase

Paseo de la Isla

Paseo del Empecinado

Further down the road there is a large botanical garden featuring vegetable species representative of a variety of ecosystems from all over the planet, and some monumental remains, which add a romantic air to the area, such as the arches donated by the count of Castilfalé, a Renaissance fountain from the Monasterio de San Pedro de Arlanza, or the late 12th-century Romanesque front of the Iglesia de Nuestra Señora de Llana, by Cerezo de Río Tirón.

On the way back, along the other side of the river, you will walk the **Paseo del Empecinado**, named after the warrior Juan Martín Díez, commonly known as "El Empecinado" (The Stubborn One), (1784-1825), famous

for his bravery during the War of Independence, and also the **Paseo del Espoloncillo**, abreast of the Espolón and built by the French invaders on the Vega lands they had previously burnt down in 1808. From the shadow of the horse chestnut trees, you can contemplate, from a distance, the beauty of the Espolón and the Arco de Santa María, with the spires of the cathedral in the background and the weeping willows, white birches, yews and round acacias standing by the river

Paseo de la Sierra de Atapuerca

Paseo de la Quinta

Further up this side of the river, upstream, you will reach the **Paseo de la Sierra de Atapuerca**, a recent denomination that forms part of the project to create a Museum of Human Evolution in the old site of the Cavalry Barracks and, before that, the Dominican convent of Saint Paul.

Past the Plaza de Santa Teresa, featuring the Convento de las Carmelitas, the last convent founded by the Burgos saint (1582), you will reach the **Paseo de la Quinta**, originally named after the property known as the Quinta del Arzopisbo, which was converted into a park around 1868, when Timoteo Arnaiz was the mayor of Burgos —he also reformed the Paseo de la Isla and turned the Paseo del Espolón into a pedestrian area.

Today the Paseo de la Quinta is a **natural theme park**, paying homage to the vegetal and landscape wealth of the province of Burgos. A tour of the park will lead you through a variety of ecosystems, from the Mediterranean species of the southern end (junipers, pine forests, holm-oak woods...) to the deciduous

Parque de Fuentes Blancas

mixed forest of the northern end, from the willow, poplar and elm plains to the mountain beeches and pines. Our province forms part of the two large ecological areas of the peninsula: the dry, Mediterranean Iberia, and the wet Iberia of the Euro-Siberian region, each with their own ecological, floral and landscape features.

From the Parque de la Quinta you will reach the parks of **Fuente del Prior** and **Fuentes Blancas**, very popular among the people of Burgos, particularly on summer days, when the heat is mitigated by the shade of the trees and the freshness of the waters of the Arlanzón.

The **Parque del Castillo** is in a different natural context. On the sides and in the top of the hillock there is a forest of cedars, cypresses and pines, concealing the remains of a primitive castle village. From the Mirador, you will have a panoramic view of the city. A bronze guide in the handrail will help you to spot the more interesting sights.

Bandstand, Paseo del Espolón

Parque del Castillo

12

City environs

QUINTANAORTUÑO
Mansilla de Burgos
Rebolledo
Cauce marmellar
Villanueva de Río Ubierna
SOTOP
Prados
Marmellar de Arriba
Vivar del C
Ayo.
SOTRAGERO
QUINTANIL
Marmellar de Abajo
Arroyal
Páramo 965
N-623
VILLAYERI
Páramo del Arroyo
Villarmero
Monasterio de Fresdelva
Ayo. del Páramo
QUINTANADUEÑAS
Villagonzalo-Arenas
Ayo. Nales
Ayo. Arlanzón
Villatoro
BURGOS
Villalonquéjar
A-231
VILLALBILLA DE BURGOS
TARDAJOS
N-120
SAN MAMÉS DE BURGOS
Corte
Villacienzo
Quintanilla de las Carretas
Ayo. de los Cangrejos
Renuncio
Río
E-80
N-620
VILLAGONZALO-PEDERNALES
Altotero de Modúbar
ALBILLOS
N-I
VILLARIEZO
Ayo. del Carmen
Villamiel de Muñó
Ventas de Saldaña
SALDAÑA DE BURGOS
Ausines
ARCOS
SARRACÍN
Ayo. Corte
A. San Clemente
Galocha
Villanueva Matamala
La Saldañuela
Cojó
A. Sta. Mala
E-5
Valdereje
Olmosalbos
Pedrosa de Muñó
Humienta

Riocerezo
Pto. de la Brújula
981
Celada de la Torre
QUINTANAPALLA
Las Mijadas
HURONES
UILLAS
Ayo. Hurones
A-1
N-I
Ayo. de Cotar
RUBENA
Cótar
Olmos de Atapuerca
ATAPUERCA
Matagrande
1.078
Yacimiento de Atapuerca
Villalval
ORBANEJA RÍO PICO
Villafría de Burgos
CARDEÑUELA RÍO PICO
Quintanilla Riopico
Río Pico
Castañares
Zalduendo
IBEAS DE JUARROS
San Medel
N-120
El Priorato
Río
CARDEÑAJIMENO
San Millán de Juarros
Ayo. del Prado
CASTRILLO DEL VAL
Mozoncillo de Juarros
San Pedro de Cardeña
Ayo. Santa Eugenia
Ayo. Pasaderilla
Río Espinosa
CEDO DE BURGOS
Cuzcurrita de Juarros
Espinosa de Juarros
Cueva
Ayo. de Sta. María
Ayo. de
Cueva de Juarros
Modúbar de San Cibrián
Ayo. del Cerro
LOS AUSINES
Sopeña
Bugedo de Juarros
Ayo. Valdezara
Quintanilla

The Burgos area is an illustrated mosaic of history, art and nature; an area filled with interesting cultural sites inherited from the most diverse cultures. Within a radius of 15 kilometres you will be able to see prehistoric dolmens in the valleys of the rivers Pico and Vena, Roman villas and roads such as Deobrígula in Tardajos or the Vía Aquitania, Muslim mill waterways like the one running from Arlanzón to Burgos, the Camino de Santiago, with its hermitages, hospitals, monasteries, villages and historical sites in Fresdelval or Vivar del Cid. Our personal favourites are the austere and imposing Monasterio de San Pedro de Cardeña, and the world-famous prehistoric sites of the Sierra de Atapuerca.

San Pedro de Cardeña. Interior

Monasterio de San Pedro de Cardeña

Located in a small valley approximately 10 kilometres away from Burgos, along the road leading to the Paseo de la Quinta and Fuentes Blancas, and run by Cistercian monks, this is one of the oldest Benedictine monasteries in the peninsula. It was founded in the late 9th century. Soon it became well known for its economic prosperity, its religious prestige, and the cultural wealth achieved by its monks, thanks to the favour of the kings and, above all, of the Castilian counts Fernán González and his son Garci Fernández.

San Pedro de Cardeña. Romanesque tower

During the Middle Ages it was a powerful feudal agent, promoting the construction of new settlements and closely collaborating with the county's authorities. It suffered raids and fires during the campaigns of Abderramán III (circa 934), when, tradition has it, 200 monks were martyred. The history of the monastery has been linked to the person, the myth and the legend of Rodrigo Díaz de Vivar, El Cid Campeador (10).

San Pedro de Cardeña

The church that can be seen today is Gothic and dates from the 15th century. One side of the cloister and the tower is all that remains of the old structure. It underwent expansion works during the 17th and 18th centuries. The Capilla del Cid was finished in 1735, to contain the mortal remains of the hero and of his wife and relatives. A few years later, in 1759, the rest of the works were completed, giving the building its current appearance. Although Baroque in style, it is a sober structure, only interrupted, in the upper section of the main front, by a vaulted niche containing the statue of Santiago (El Cid?) Matamoros.

San Pedro de Cardeña. Claustro de los Mártires

The visit to the archaeological sites of the Sierra de Atapuerca can start at Ibeas de Juarros or Atapuerca. There are reception points for visitors in both towns, as well as interpretation rooms and car park facilities. Visits are guided.

Archaeological sties of the Sierra de Atapuerca

The archaeological sites of the Sierra de Atapuerca are located 15 km east of Burgos, at a smooth hillock straddled between the mountains of the Sistema Ibérico and the Cordillera Cantábrica. It is the largest prehistoric site in the world, containing 70% of the fossils of the Mid Pleistocene period, according to the experts.

Of particular interest are the *Gran Dolina* site, where a series of hominid fossils, the oldest in Europe, belonging to a new human species, the Homo Antecessor, have been found –this species lived more than 800,000 years ago–, and the site known as the *Sima de los Huesos* (Chasm of Bones), where the most complete collection of bones has been found, around 3,000 human fossils corresponding to thirty-two 300,000-year-old pre-Neardenthal individuals of both sexes and different ages.

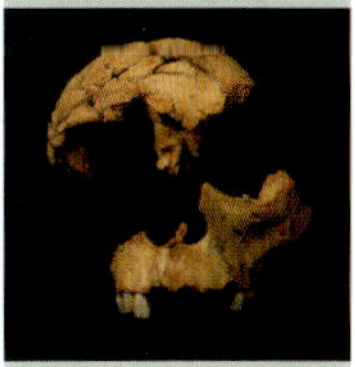

Recently they have been declared World Sites by UNESCO. The construction in Burgos of the Museo de la Evolución Humana will make available to the general public the scientific findings of a series of sites that, despite the objects found, still contain many answers to the questions on human evolution.

Fiestas
cuisine and shopping

FIESTAS MAYORES DE SAN PEDRO Y SAN PABLO

June 29

During these big fiestas, which last between 7 and 10 days, the city is transformed and decorated, and a plethora of festive, cultural and traditional events take place in the city streets. June 29 is the big day.

Until 1873, the Fiestas Mayores of the city were held during the month of September, once the farming activities had been completed and coinciding with the Fiesta de la Exaltación de la Santa Cruz. In 1873 a Celebrations Committee was formed and the fiestas were moved to the month of June.

Today, the fiestas feature a varied programme of activities, and there is something for each sector of the population.

Among the more traditional events are:

- Opening speech and proclamation of the Queens of the fiestas
- Offering of flowers to Santa María la Mayor, the city's matron saint
- Floats parade
- Singing of the Burgos anthem at the Paseo del Espolón

- Parade of *gigantillos*, *gigantones* and *danzantes* through the city streets.

Among the most popular activities are:

- Fireworks sessions and competition
- Concerts by top artists in the national and international music scene
- Open-air dances
- Sports competitions
- Street performances
- Bullfighting

There are also shows for children, circus, puppets, interactive games, etc.

The dances and activities for the elderly, plus all sorts of exhibitions and varied cultural manifestations, complete the fiestas programme, which every year becomes more and more interactive.

"Día de las Peñas" or "Día del Burgalés ausente"

This celebration has been declared an Event of Regional Interest

It takes place on the last Sunday of the Fiestas de San Pedro y San Pablo in the city of Burgos.

From early in the morning, thousands of people gather at the Parque de Fuentes Blancas, 5 km away from the city centre.

On that day homage is paid to all the *burgaleses ausentes* (natives of Burgos living abroad). By means of the so-called Operación Añoranza (Operation Homesickness), a group of Burgos people living abroad is invited to enjoy the fiestas and, on the last day, share a picnic day with the people of Burgos.

From early in the morning, the *peñas* (local folk clubs) and the Regional Houses set up stands in the Parque de las Fuentes Blancas. After a mass celebrated by the Capilla de la Virgen del Álamo begins the Concurso Gastronómico del Buen Yantar, a cuisine competition that contributes to exalting the Burgos cuisine and typical local products. The *peñas* offer gastronomic products and the fiesta goes on until dusk, with dances and activities for everybody.

This is the finishing touch of the Fiestas de San Pedro y San Pablo.

The protagonists

Gigantillos

The *gigantillos* (small giants) are two friendly popular characters made of papier mâché that parade during the city's fiestas. Created in 1899, they were destroyed by a fire in 1973 and recovered later on, at the initiative of the City Hall. They represent a mountain couple that dances along with the *pasacalles* (informal street troupes) of Corpus Christi, Curpillos and the Fiestas de San Pedro. They are among the more dearly loved characters in Burgos.

Gigantones

Five giant figures representing the different races of the world. Like the *gigantillos*, they were destroyed by a fire in 1973. Their height varies between 3.76 and 4 m, and they weigh between 60 and 72 kg. A new couple of *gigantones* –representing El Cid and his wife Jimena– was introduced in 1984.

Danzantes

A group of dancing children dressed in the old style of the Court. They participate in the *pasacalles* of the most important fiestas in the city.

Tetines

They accompany the *danzantes*, and their origin dates back to an extravagantly dressed grotesque character that represented the sins and the devil and used to scare away the people of Burgos, who made fun of him and called him names. They wear colourful costumes, with conical hats, and hold a horse's tail in their hands, whipping away along the streets as they flee from the Santísimo. The *tetines* accompany the *danzantes*; one of them, always dressed in blue, is the master of dances; the other three accompany and organise the group of *danzantes*.

CURPILLOS

The first Friday after Corpus Christi.

This fiesta takes place at the Monasterio de las Huelgas Reales, the Huelgas quarter and the Parque del Parral.

The origins of the Curpillos tradition in Burgos are linked to the victory of Alfonso VI in the battle of Navas de Tolosa, on July 16, 1212. After several changes of date, it was agreed to celebrate this fiesta on the first Friday following Corpus Christi.

It has two clearly differentiated parts: the more solemn acts, which are held during the first hours of the fiesta, and the popular part, which takes place in the Parque del Parral, with the participation of all the present.

The fiesta begins with the gathering and formation of the military troops prior to the mass held in the Monasterio de las Huelgas. The abbess of the monastery receives the civil and military authorities. After the Eucharist, a procession sets out, featuring *gigantones* and *danzantes*, the pennant of Navas de Tolosa carried by the military of the highest rank in the city, the archbishop holding the Santísimo under a pallium, and the civil authorities escorted by the police in gala dress. Once the troops have paraded and the *gigantones* and *danzantes* have danced before the authorities, the fiesta continues in the nearby Parque del Parral.

The people of Burgos take over the fiesta at El Parral. The shaded park is the perfect venue for this gathering of locals and strangers, who come to taste the dishes cooked in the stands set up by the *peñas* and regional houses. The flea market set up near the park and the public dances add colour and sound to this fiesta, which ends late in the evening.

The protagonists

Pendón de las Navas de Tolosa

This pennant is a precious trophy taken from the Arabs during the battle of the same name, which took place in 1212, and kept in the monastery. It is the best existing piece of Almohade tapestry. It is woven with gold, silver and silks, measures 3.30 x 2 m, and has an inscription with references to Allah, within a star surrounding another central star. It is thought to have been an ornament at the entrance of the tent of the sultan Abú-Yasuf-Jacub, known as Miramamolín.

It was restored in 1953, and since then the highest military authority in the city carries a replica of this precious piece of tapestry during the Curpillos procession.

SAN LESMES

Celebrated on the Sunday closest to January 30th.

This fiesta honours the city's patron saint, San Lesmes, who arrived in the city with the king Alfonso VI and dedicated his life to caring for the pilgrims of the Camino de Santiago in the Monasterio de San Juan, of which he was abbot.

His French background led to the town-twinning between Burgos and the saint's hometown, Loudun. Every year, a group of representative authorities from this town come to Burgos to celebrate this fiesta.

On San Lesmes' day, the municipal corporation, together with the guest authorities from Loudun, walk, escorted by guards in gala uniform, from the Casa Consistorial to the Iglesia de San Lesmes, accompanied by the *gigantillos* and some folk groups. Upon reaching the church, the Mayor, as the highest municipal authority and in representation of all the people of Burgos, offers a candle and the traditional *panecillos* (bread buns) to the Saint. After this religious act, the fiesta continues at the Plaza de San Juan, with stands selling *chorizo* (red sausage), *morcilla* (blood sausage), wine, and the famous *panecillos* offered to the saint.

Concerts, exhibits and cultural and sport events take place before and after this celebration.

OTHER CELEBRATIONS

■ Romería de Nuestra Señora la Blanca

Date: last week-end of May

This pilgrimage is closely linked to the castle and its recovery. Next to the splendorous Burgos fortress used to stand a Romanesque church containing the image of Nuestra Señora de la Blanca. That church, one of the most important in the city, was destroyed, together with the castle, in 1813.

The castle's park is a privileged natural space due to its closeness to the city. A project to recover the area was put in place in 1993: the goal of the so-called Plan Especial del Castillo (Special Castle Plan) is to turn the area into an archaeological park, featuring a centre for the interpretation of the fortress and an exceptional lookout to contemplate the city's old quarter. Throughout 1994, with a view to disseminating the process of recovery of the castle, a number of guided and educational visits were organised, which culminated with the celebration of a Romería in honour of the Virgen Blanca: a procession carried the image of the Virgin from the Iglesia de San Pedro de la Fuente to the open field where the remains of the original church are located. The last week-end of the month of May was the date chosen for this celebration, a tradition that has been kept throughout the years.

The medieval world, in which the castle belongs, was closely linked to this pilgrimage from its inception. The main programmed acts are the medieval market –featuring music

concerts, street performances, workshops, horseback jousting, etc.– and the pilgrimage, which takes place on Sunday, with an invariably massive participation of people, who gather at the open field and enjoy the thousands of portions of paella distributed among the present, in a traditional country atmosphere.

Carnavales

Carnival takes place during the days prior to Ash Wednesday, when Lent begins. During those days all the pleasures and vices of life are indulged in, in clear opposition to the austerity that will prevail until the end of Easter.

This celebration was reborn during the Middle Ages, due to the radical Lent obligations imposed by the Church, including fasting and a strict abstinence.

Today Carnival means popular fun and people in costumes.

Tarasca, *Chamarrones* and *Cachidiablos* are the protagonists of this fiesta, representing Sin and the Devil scaring people away. It begins on the last Thursday before Ash Wednesday and ends on Carnival Tuesday with the Burial of the Sardine.

El Obispillo

Recovered after many years of oblivion, this fiesta is held on December 28th, the Day of the Innocent Saints. Children are the protagonists of this celebration, which starts a few days before the Day of the Innocent Saints, with the election of El Obispillo among the Pueri Cantores, that is, the members of the cathedral's boys choir. On that day, the boy chosen as El Obispillo walks through the city streets handing out sweets to the children. He visits the City Hall and is received by the Mayor, in whose company he greets the people of Burgos from the balcony of the Casa Consistorial.

Semana Santa
Event of Regional Interest

Holy Week is characterised by the solemnity of its processions.

Among the more outstanding acts of this fiesta are the Procesión del Encuentro (Procession of the Meeting), on Good Thursday, and the penitential Via Crucis at the castle.

CUISINE

Ibeas beans

Burgos blood sausage

Postre del abuelo ("Grandpa's dessert", consisting of Burgos fresh cheese)

Lamb's feet

As befits a region traditionally dedicated to produce everything necessary to meet the alimentary needs of its population, today Burgos boasts a select, age-long cuisine that will satisfy the most exquisite palates.

The staple products of Burgos cuisine are the top-quality bread, wine and meat from the local cereal fields, vineyards, orchards and farms, most of them family-run operations, spread throughout the region.

The white **bread**, eaten dry, in soup or as a dessert, and the prestigious **wine** from Ribera de Duero and the banks of the river Arlanza, contribute the necessary and unquestionably delicious calories. The legume and vegetable ***potajes*** (broths) enjoy a well-deserved fame; the red beans from Ibeas, the *caparrones* (buds) from Belorado, the lentils from the high moors, the chickpeas…

As to **meat** dishes, the options increase considerably. Particularly tasty is the roasted or stewed ***lechazo*** (young lamb), today's version of the proverbial mutton and beef eaten in the past by a population almost exclusively dedicated to cattle-raising and farming activities. The same can be said of pork meat, carefully selected after the ritual **slaughtering of the pigs** that takes place among the country families, an essential meat for the preparation of traditional stews such as the *olla podrida* (Spanish stew) and other popular dishes such as the *chorizo cocido* (boiled red sausage), *picadillo* (mince), *torrezno* (rasher) or **Burgos *morcilla*** (blood sausage).

Other equally tasty products are the beef, ox, lamb or sheep *cecina* (dry meat), an ideal alternative to fresh meat, or the famous **Burgos cheese**, which, eaten plain or with sugar, honey or quince jelly and walnuts, is known as the ***postre del abuelo*** (grandpa's dessert), to be consumed preferably at the end of a good meal.

The local game and fish products add variety and richness to the traditional cuisine; in fact, the province of Burgos is full of forests and valleys, meadows and rivers. Depending on the season, you can eat autochthonous delicacies such as quail, partridge, rabbit, hare, wild boar and deer, in the meat department, as well as the Arlanzón, Arlanza or Pedroso trout, in the fish department. There is also the river crab, currently in the middle of a repopulation process after a crisis that put in danger the most emblematic crustaceous of Burgos cuisine.

Other traditional products featured in the local cuisine are **fungi** and **mushrooms** –*perrechicos*, thistle and *carrerilla* mushrooms, *níscalos*– and **watercress**, used in salad and as garnishing.

Trout salad

Finally, the local **fruit** –cherries from Covarrubias or the Valle de las Caderechas, apples, plums, pears from the eastern and northern valleys of the province– and the **sweets** made with traditional techniques –almonds from Briviesca, *empiñonados* (pine nut pastry) from Aranda, *yemas* (egg-yolk sweet) from Burgos, plus other homemade sweets lovingly prepared by the enclosed nuns in the Calatrava, Clarisian, and Salesian convents, among others– complete a rich, varied and delicious menu.

Fresh cheese ice-cream

It is up to you to enjoy it at any of the many local restaurants, offering a select variety of dishes. Entrees consisting of Castilian or garlic soup, *morcilla* and *chorizo* skewers, *cecina*, *manitas* (pork trotters), vegetable and mushroom mixed dishes, *potajes*, *olla podrida*, ox's tail and potatoes, trout from the river Arlanzón, roasted *lechazo*, chops, stewed game, stewed hare, *leche frita* (fried milk), Burgos cheese, *cuajada* (curd), *arroz con leche* (rice pudding), hard cheeses... In addition to all this, the area's closeness to the sea and the culinary wealth of the surrounding provinces contribute new products and ideas, making Burgos cuisine a traditional and modern one, able to satisfy the palate of the most demanding gourmet.

Lamb chops

Roasted lamb

SHOPPING

Burgos is a shopping city; a large shop-window where you can find everything, from the typical gastronomic products –*morcilla*, cheese, wines from Ribera del Duero and the banks of the river Arlanza, *lechazo*, fruits and vegetables, crafts– to the latest fashion and jewellery trends and cutting-edge technologies, combining the modern shops located in exclusively commercial areas with the small family-run shops scattered throughout the city.

In fact, the life and the economy of this city have traditionally revolved around its commercial activity, which reached its heyday in the 16th century, thanks to the trading –mainly of ship's wool– with the Netherlands, managed by the Consulado del Mar.

Commerce in Burgos is a blend of tradition and modernity. It is a dynamic commerce, which has undergone a quick evolution during the last few years, due in good part to the implementation of the Global Plan for the Support of Commerce created by the City Hall and the Federation of Associations of Tradesmen, which has led to the modernisation not only of many existing establishments, but of the management, training and specialisation of the tradespeople and the consolidation of a number of commercial zones as open recreational and leisure spaces.

In addition to the rich and dynamic network of traditional shops, the city has three large commercial centres and three municipal markets –South, North and G-9–, although there is a predominance of the small, high-quality shops, grouped by sectors and spaces. The Trading Associations play a fundamental role in the social structure of Burgos. Burgos has four eminently commercial areas –Centro Histórico, Gamonal, Zona Bernardas and Zona Sur– with a highly diversified offer: boutiques, shoe-shops, bookshops, jewellery shops and perfumeries: and everything is handy, without big crowds, without hassles, so you can fully enjoy your shopping.

A wide variety of cultural and leisure activities complete the appealing city offer. Burgos hosts a plethora of congresses and meetings on many different topics. In the future, the city's cultural infrastructure will be expanded, with projects such as the Museo de la Evolución Humana and the Auditorio. Burgos's academic and cosmopolitan nature can be seen in its streets and in its prolific cultural agenda.

FESTIVALS AND CULTURAL ACTIVITIES

Festival Internacional de Folklore

The Festival Internacional de Folklore begins in July, right after the Fiestas Mayores. It is one of the most important international festivals of its kind, having already reached its 26th edition. The streets are filled with colour and music, encouraging people to participate in the folklore and culture of other countries.

This festival is a reference and a model of cultural exchange and universal fraternity.

Estío Musical

During a whole week at the end of August, classical music becomes the main feature in the programming of the Teatro Principal.

EnClave de Calle

In September, the streets become the stage for this international festival of the arts, with the participation of leading companies, offering innovative shows for all publics.

Festival Internacional de Teatro Escena Abierta

This theatre festival features shows representative of the latest trends in the stage-performing arts. It is held in January (since 2000) and includes performances by national and international companies. Besides the theatre shows, there are also parallel activities such as exhibitions and workshops. The performances are held in the Teatro Principal and the Teatro Clunia in Burgos. The festival is organised by the Municipal Institute for Culture of the Burgos City Hall and the university de Burgos (Vice-Rectorate of Students and University Extension. Theatre Workshop).

THEATRES

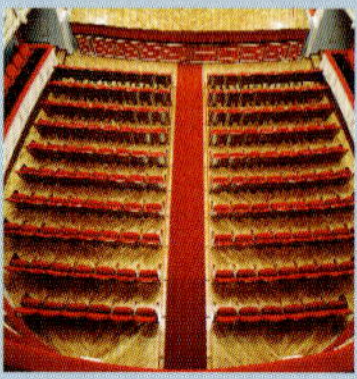

Teatro Principal

An Isabelline-style edifice inaugurated in 1858, whose cultural activity lasted until 1946, when it was closed due to its ruinous condition. It was reopened on July 7th, 1997, after a successful refurbishing process, which reactivated the city's cultural life with a stable and continuous program of activities. Today, it continues to play a key role in Burgos. It seats 900 people.

In the same building are an exhibition room, a library, a reception hall (Salón Rojo) and a lecture room (Sala Polisón) with a capacity of 180.

Tel. 947 288873
Instituto Municipal de Cultura 947 288840
Cultural information: AFORO magazine and www.aytoburgos.es

Teatro Clunia

It occupies part of the old Alhóndiga Municipal built in 1514. Its subsequent use as a gaol changed the structure of the building, which today has been converted into a cultural centre named after Francisco Salinas.

Programme: "Las noches de Clunia" are aimed at a public that enjoys watching innovative and contemporary performing-art shows. It has been recently refurbished and seats 600 people.
Tel. 947 203040

EXHIBITION ROOMS

Monasterio de San Juan

Old monastery of the 15th and 16th centuries, featuring the original cloister, chapter room, and the ruins of the church. Today, it promotes an intense cultural activity: exhibitions, lectures, congresses, musical soirées, etc. Since 1968, it holds the best works by the Burgos painter Marceliano Santamaría, in the museum bearing his name.
Opening hours: Tuesday through Saturday 11.00 am to 2.00 pm. and 5.00 pm. to 8.00 pm.
Sundays: 10.00 am to 2.00 pm.
Mondays and holidays: closed.
Address: Pza. San Juan s/n
Tel. 947 205687

Arco de Santa María

16th-century historic-artistic edifice standing at one of the wall gates. It conserves the

old meeting room of the Council of Burgos, the Sala de Poridad, and its main hall features a mural painting by Vela Zanetti and the pharmacy of the old Hospital de San Juan.
Opening hours: Weekdays 11.00 am to 3.00 pm and 5.00 pm to 8.50 pm.
Sundays: 11.00 am to 2.00 pm.
Mondays and holidays: closed.
Address: Pza. del Rey San Fernando s/n
Tel. 947 288868

Centro de Arte Contemporáneo

In the upper part of the city, in harmony with the streets and monuments of the old quarter, stands the Centro de Arte Caja Burgos (CAB), showing the permanent collection of contemporary art that the savings bank Caja Burgos started in the 1990's. The collection includes works by the most important and active artists of the last decade, with very open selection criteria in terms of supports and tendencies, which allows visitors to see paintings and sculptures next to video art, photographs and installations.

The CAB also holds temporary exhibits and encourages innovative and interactive artistic creation, since it has been conceived as an activating centre and as a meeting space for all sorts of contemporary cultural manifestations.
www.cabdeburgos.com

ARCHIVES AND LIBRARIES

Archivo Municipal. Palacio de Castilfalé

Located in an old 16th-century palace, the municipal archives contain documents concerned with the history of the city and the City Hall dating from as early as the 12th century

to the present. It has a vast and interesting graphic collection as well as a library specialised in Burgos-related topics.
Opening hours: Monday through Friday 8.30 am to 2.30 pm.
Address: C/ Fernán González, 56
Information and visits tel. 947 288812
E-mail: archivo@aytoburgos.es

Archivo Provincial. Monasterio de San Agustín

Recently restored by the Diputación Provincial, this old monastery holds the provincial archives. Among the most interesting remains of the old monastery is the 13th-century cloister area, with its lecture and exhibition halls.

Library opening hours: 11.00 am to 2.00 pm and 5.00 pm to 9 pm.
Archives opening hours: 9 am to 2 pm.
Address: C/ Madrid
Tel. 947 255758

Biblioteca Municipal Gonzalo de Berceo

Opening hours: Monday through Friday 9.00 am to 9.00 pm, Saturdays 9.30 am to 2.00 pm.
Address: C/ Pedro Alfaro, s/n
E-mail: biblioteca@aytoburgos.es

Biblioteca Municipal Teatro Principal

Opening hours: Monday through Friday 9.00 am to 9.00 pm, Saturdays 9.30 am to 2.00 pm.
Address: Teatro principal. Paseo del Espolón, s/n

Biblioteca Municipal M.ª Teresa León

Address: Plaza Sierra Nevada, s/n

HOTELS

LANDA PALACE *****
Ctra. N-I, Km. 235
VILLAGONZALO-PEDERNALES (Burgos)
Tel: 947 257777

ABBA BURGOS ****
Fernán González, 72-76
Tel: 947 001100

AC BURGOS ****
Avda. de la Isla, 7
Tel: 947 257966

CORONA DE CASTILLA ****
Madrid, 15
Tel: 947 262142

FERNAN GONZALEZ ****
Calera, 17
Tel: 947 209441

NH PALACIO DE LA MERCED ****
Merced, 13
Tel: 947 479900

PUERTA DE BURGOS ****
Vitoria, 69
Tel: 947 241000

RICE ****
Avda. Reyes Católicos, 30
Tel: 947 222300

VELADA BURGOS ****
Fernán González, 6
Tel: 947 257680

ARLANZÓN ***
Bonifacio Zamora de Usabel, 1 A
Tel: 947 257 633

CASA AZOFRA ***
Don Juan de Austria, 22
Tel: 947 461050 / 947 462003

LA VARGA ***
Ctra. N-I, km. 232
VILLAGONZALO-PEDERNALES (Burgos)
Tel: 947 201640

DEL CID ***
Plaza Santa María, 8
Tel: 947 208715

MESON DEL CID II ***
Fernán González, 62
Tel: 947 208715

TIZONA ***
Severo Ochoa, 7 Bis
Tel: 947 234123

ABC LANDILLA **
Ctra. Madrid-Irún, km. 235
VILLAGONZALO PEDERNALES (Burgos)
Tel: 947 209003

AREA CASTIL **
Ctra. N-I, km. 233
VILLAGONZALO-PEDERNALES (Burgos)
Tel: 947 206860

ESPAÑA **
Paseo del Espolón, 32
Tel: 947 206340

HARO **
Condes de Castilfalé, 1-3
Tel: 947 462158

PUERTA ROMEROS **
San Amaro, 2.
Tel: 947 460738

VILLA JIMENA **
Paseo de los Pisones, 47
Tel: 947 207430

HOSTELS

ALMIRANTE BONIFAZ ****
Vitoria, 22 y 24
Tel: 947 206943

CABILDO***
Avda. del Cid, 2 bis
Tel: 947 257840

CARDEÑA ***
San Pedro Cardeña, 50
Tels: 947 491780 / 947 491781

CORDÓN ***
La Puebla, 6.
Tel: 947 265000

LA PUEBLA ***
C/ La Puebla, 20
Tel: 947 200011

MARIA LUISA ***
Avda. Cid Campeador, 42
Tel: 947 228000

ABC CONDE DE MIRANDA **
Miranda, 4
Tel: 947 265267

BUENOS AIRES **
Ctra. N-I, km. 245
VILLAFRÍA (Burgos)
Tel: 947 483770

NORTE Y LONDRES **
Pl. Alonso Martínez, 10
Tel: 947 264125

VEGAS, LAS **
Ctra. N-I, km. 245
VILLAFRÍA (Burgos)
Tel: 947 484453

JACOBEO *
San Juan, 24.
Tel: 947 260102

LAR **
Cardenal Benlloch, 1
Tel: 947 209655

JOMA *
San Juan, 26-2°
Tel: 947 203350

VILLAHOZ *
Los Corrales, 15
(Barrio de Villalonquéjar)
Tel: 947 298598

ACACIA **
Bernabé Pérez Ortiz, 1
Tel: 947 205134

ACANTO **
Esteban Saez Alvarado, 3
Tel: 947 482551

ALCÁNTARA **
Villadiego, 16
Tel: 947 463211

ARLANZÓN **
Vitoria, 242-1°
Tel: 947 470369

CARRALES **
Puente Gasset, 4
Tel: 947 205916

EVOLUCIÓN **
Santa Clara, 28
Tel: 947 256077

HILTON **
Vitoria, 165-1°
Tel: 947 225116

JUARREÑO **
Santa Clara, 29
Tel: 947 265038

MANJÓN **
Gran Teatro, 1-7
Tel: 947 208689

LAS TERRAZAS **
Ctra. Burgos-Aguilar, Km. 4
Tel: 947 270205

LA TESORERA **
Vitoria, 79.
Tel: 947 223592

SANTIAGO 2 **
Vicente Alexandre, 6
Tels: 947 052607 / 947 046230

GARCÍA *
Santander, 1-3° Dcha.
Tel: 947 205553

HIDALGO *
Almirante Bonifaz, 14-1° Izda.
Tel: 947 203481

TEMIÑO *
Concepción, 14-Esc. Dcha. 1° Izda. Tel: 947 208035

TORRES *
Vitoria, 178-1°
Tel: 947 222416

196
Vitoria, 196-1°
Tel: 947 229474

ABEDUL
Cardenal Benlloch, 3 - 4°
Tel: 947 205134

ANA
Juan de Austria, 8
Tel: 619 267784

ARRIBAS
Oviedo, 8.
Tel: 947 266292

BELLA VISTA
Villadiego, s/n
Tel: 947 460222

DALLAS
Pl.Vega, 6 - 1°
Tel: 947 205457

DIONI
Arzobispo de Castro, 2 - 1°
Tel: 947 241847

EL PESQUERO
Avda. de la Constitución, 21-1°
Tel: 947 240950

IBEAS
Pedro Alfaro, 2 - 5°
Tel: 947 484437

LA ISLA
Villalón, 9 - 4° F
Tel: 947 273804

JOEL
Avda. Constitución Española, 3 y 5.
Tel: 947 225009

JUAN XXIII
Lavaderos, 21
Tel: 947 221739

LAR DOS
Cardenal Benlloch, 1 - 7°
Tel: 947 209655

MIAMI
Vitoria, 53 bis
Tel: 947 271041

NUMANCIA III
María Moliner, 10
Tel: 947 474008

PARDO
Santa Bárbara, 20 - 1°
Tel: 947 223938

PEÑA
Puebla, 18
Tel: 947 206323

PUNTA BRAVA
Paseo Fuentecillas, 3 - 5°
Tel: 947 208211

SANTIAGO
Santiago, 8 bis
Tel: 947 046230

SEDANO
Avda. Cid Campeador, 45
Tel: 947 221076

VICTORIA
San Juan, 3 - 2°
Tel: 947 201542

RESTAURANTS

AC BURGOS
Avda. de la Isla, 7
Tel: 947 257966

ARANCHA
Puente Gasset, 4
Tel: 947 208895

ARCOS DEL PARRAL
Condes de Castilfalé, 7
Tel: 947 229990

ARRIBAS
Oviedo, 6
Tel: 947 266292

ARLANZA
Córdoba, 4
Tel: 947 487438

ASADOR CASA AZOFRA
Don Juan de Austria, 22-24
Tel: 947 461050

ASADOR DE ARANDA
Llana de Afuera, s/n
Tel: 947 268141

ASADOR HORNO PARRILLA
Camino Casa la Vega, 43
Tel: 947 272580

ASADOR LAS BRASAS
Calzadas, 10
Tel: 947 272580

ASADOR LAS CALZADAS
Calzadas, 7
Tel: 947 272384

ASADOR LOS TRILLOS
Don Juan de Austria, 20
Tel: 947 460026

ASADOR SAN LORENZO
Crta. Poza, 79B 1
Tel: 947 474733

ASTORGA
Avellanos, 8
Tel: 947 206182

ASTUR
Regino Sáiz de la Maza, 2
Tel: 947 200564

ATELIER DE COCINA
Jesús María Ordoño, 4
Tel: 687 279045

AVELINO
Emperador, 58
Tel: 947 206192

AVENIDA
Avda. Cid, 92.
Tel: 947 221022

BARQUIN
Camino de Burgos, s/n
(B° de Villalonquéjar)
Tel: 947 298024

BELLA VISTA
Villadiego, s/n
Tel: 947 460222

BIG BOLERA
Soria, s/n.
Tel: 947 244747

BNB
Parque del Castillo, s/n
Tel: 947 266259

BODEGÓN EL PEREGRINO
Fernán González, 48
Tel: 947 205547

BONFÍN
Cadena y Eleta, 1
Tel: 947 206193

BUENOS AIRES
Ctra. N-I, Km. 245
VILLAFRÍA (Burgos)
Tel: 947 483770

CAESAR
Briviesca, 20
Tel: 947 277626

CAMPING FUENTES BLANCAS
Crta. Fuentes Blancas, s/n
Tel: 947 483480

CANDELAS
Las Candelas, 9
Tel: 947 471896

CANTARES
Avda. Constitución, 35
Tel: 947 221193

CAÑAS Y TAPAS
Padre Aramburu, 13
Tel: 947 236648

CARMEN
Vitoria, 191
Tel: 947 221017

CASA AGOTE
Federico Martínez Varea, 7
Tel: 947 228813

CASA FELIPE
Madrid, 70
Tel: 947 277166

CASA GERARDO
Trujillo, 3
Tel: 947 470453

CASA MARTÍN
Burgense, 12
Tel: 947 200170

CASA MARCELO
Plaza San Bruno, 1
Tel: 947 235752

CASA OJEDA
Vitoria, 5
Tel: 947 209052

CASINO
Paseo del Espolón, 26
Tel: 947 278156

CONDE DE MIRANDA
Miranda, 4
Tel: 947 265267

CONTINENTAL
Pza. del Doctor López Sáiz, 4
Tel: 947 204679

CORAZAS
Calzadas, 24-26
Tel: 947 202047

COPACABANA
Avda. de la Constitución Española, 1
Tel: 947 227199

DE SIMÓN
Marqués de Berlanga, 2
Tel: 947 044847

DOGO
Vitoria, 202
Tel: 947 230459

DON MENÚ
Vitoria, 202
Tel: 947 230459

ANTONIO DON JAMÓN
San Pablo, 3
Tel: 947 265661

DON JAMÓN
Alvar García, s/n
Tel: 947 272872

DON NUÑO
Nuño Rasura, 3
Tel: 947/200373

EL COMPÁS DE HUELGAS
Alfonso VIII, 39
Tel: 947 261585

EL PESQUERO
Avda. de la Constitución, 21-1°
Tel: 947 240950

EL GRECO
Madrid, 32
Tel: 947 265302

EL PORTÓN DE BURGOS
Vitoria, 69
Tel: 947 281011

EL SEGOVIANO
Clunia, 11
Tel: 947 229990

EL 24 DE LA PALOMA
Paloma, 24
Tel: 947 208608

EL SILO
Plza. Avelino Antolín Toledano, 7
Tel: 947 486206

ÉPOCA
Avda. de la Paz, 43
Tel: 947 230005

ESPOLÓN
Paseo del Espolón, s/n
Tel: 947 279976

F. IBÁÑEZ
Calatravas 3
Tel: 947 265914

FUENTE DEL PRIOR
Crta. de Fuentes Blancas, s/n
Tel: 947 276660

FUENTES BLANCAS
Parque Fuentes Blancas
Tel: 947 471158

GAMBRINUS
Avda Cantabria, 51
Tel: 947 225313

GAMONAL
Vitoria, 191
Tel: 947 220036

GAONA
La Paloma, 41
Tel: 947 204032

HARO
Condés de Castilfalé, 1-3
Tel: 947 462158

HERMANOS ALONSO
Llana de Afuera, 5
Tel: 947 201711

HOGAR DE LA RIOJA
Laín Calvo, 39
Tel: 947 202931

IBEAS
Candelas, 21
Tel: 947 220009

IN VINO VERITAs
San Lorenzo, 35
Tel: 947 200992

IRACHE
San Agustín, 3
Tel: 947 203676

IRUÑAKO
Ctra. N-I, Km. 245
VILLAFRÍA (Burgos)
Tel: 947 486265

JAMÓN JAMÓN, RESTAURANTE IBÉRICO
Avda. Eladio Perlado, 13
Tel: 947 489529

JAVI
Jesús María Ordoño, 4
Tel: 947 270455

JESÚS
Ctra. N-I, Km. 245 - Villafría
Tel: 947 225031

JORGE
Santa Casilda, 4
Tel: 947 272047

JUARREÑO
Vitoria, 182
Tel: 947 213490

KERSYN
Parque Virgen del Manzano, 10
Tel: 662 519651

LA CASA DE LAS FLORES
Avda. Reyes Católicos, 49-51
Tels: 947 225630 / 947 257190

LA FÁBULA
Puebla, 18
Tel: 947 263092

LA ABBADIA
Fernán González, 72
Tel: 947 001100

LA FAVORITA TABERNA URBANA
Avellano, 8
Tel: 947 205949

LA GLORIA
Puerta Romeros, 1
Tel: 947 205950

LA CITY
Briviesca, 4
Tel: 947 275526

LA PARADA DE HUELGAS
Alfonso VIII, 39
Tel: 947 261585

LA COARTADA
Avda. de los Reyes Católicos, 43
Tel: 645 817172

LA POSADA
Santo Domingo de Guzmán, 18
Tel: 947 204578

LA LEYENDA
Trujillo, 8
Tel: 628 716173

LA POSADA DEL CID
Plaza de Santa María, 4
Tel: 947 274930

LA MARÍA
Don Juan de Austria, 10
Tel: 947 205154

LA PEDRAJA
Avda. Constitución Española, 76
Tel: 947 244123

LA PLANCHA
Ctra. Poza, 87
Tel: 947 480393

LA RIOJANA
Avellanos, 10
Tel: 947 206132

LA SAL
Avda del Vena, 6
Tel: 947 225253

LA SARTÉN DE TOÑO
Pza.Virgen del Manzano, 10
947 481227

LA TABERNA
DEL MIRADOR
Ctra. Santander, Km. 2
Tel: 947 231513

LA TABERNA DE TANIN II
Doctor Fleming, 7
Tel: 947 279999

LA TABERNA DEL BARRIO
Ctra. Poza, 5 Bajo
Tel: 947 483120

LAS CUATRO TORRES SUR
Calatravas, 3
Tel: 947 265914

LA TAHONA
Calera, 9
Tel: 947 275644

LA TAPITA
Ávila, 2 bajo.
Tel: 947 260401

LA TESORERA
Vitoria, 79.
Tel: 947 220011

LA TOSCA
Laín Calvo, 48
Tel: 947 266735

LA TRÉBEDE
Guiomar Fernández, 14
Tel: 947 225086

LA VILLA DE ALMANZOR
Pablo Casals, 25
Tel: 947 232452

LANDA PALACE
Crta. N-I, km. 235
VILLAGONZALO-
PEDERNALES (Burgos)
Tel: 947 206343

LANDILLA
Crta. N-I, km. 235
VILLAGONZALO-
PEDERNALES (Burgos)
Tel: 947 209003

LAS TERRAZAS
Ctra. Burgos Aguilar, km 4
Tel: 947 292621

LAS VEGAS
Ctra. N-I, Km. 245
VILLAFRÍA (Burgos)
Tel: 947 484453

LA VIEJA CASTILLA
Carmen, 6
Tel: 947 201149

LAS VEGUILLAS
Pº de la Quinta, s/n
Tel: 947 275376

LÓPEZ
Alcalde Martín Cobos, 5
Tel: 947 230001

LOS FAROLES
Mérida, 9
Tel: 947 484410

LOS SAUCES
Vitoria, 22-24
Tel: 947 206848

MANRIQUE
San Lesmes, 2
Tel: 947 208742

MANZANEDO
Avda. de la Constitución
Española, 21
Tel: 947 240950

MARISCOS PIÑEIRO
Santiago, 2 bis
Tel: 947 233862

MARISCOS PIÑEIRO
Morco, 6
Tel: 947 272153

MARCI
Avda. del Cid, 86
Tel: 947 221058

MARGARITA
Travesía de la Iglesia, 3
Tel: 947 489146

MAYORAL
San Pablo, 16
Tel: 947 266130

MAYTE
Avda. del Cid, 81
Tel: 947 226239

MELCHOR
La Ventosa, 6
Tel: 947 205965

MESÓN BURGOS
Sombrerería, 8
Tel: 947 206150

MESÓN DE
LOS INFANTES
Paseo de la Isla, 2
Tel: 947 205982

MESÓN DEL CID
Plaza de Santa María, 8
Tel: 947 205971

MESÓN DEL CID II
Fernán González, 62
Tel: 947 208715

MESÓN DEL VENA
Antonio Machado, 4
Tel: 947 221551

MESÓN EL CAMINO
Villadiego, s/n
Tel: 947 273426

MESÓN EL LAUREL
Pza. San Bruno, 14
Tel: 947 223647

MESÓN JUAN XXIII
Lavaderos, 21
Tel: 947 221739

MESÓN LA CATEDRAL
Fernán González, 46
Tel: 947 274388

MESÓN LA CUEVA
Pza. Santa María, 7
Tel: 947 208671

MESÓN LA PIEDRA
San Pedro y San Felices, 45
Tel: 947 268925

MESÓN LOS HERREROS
San Lorenzo, 20
Tel: 947 202448

MIAMI
Vitoria, 53
Tel: 947 271406

MIGUEL
Serramagna, 3
Tel: 947 277181

MONTAÑÉS
Don Juan de Austria, 10
Tel: 947 205154

MOYPI
Dª Berenguela, 1
Tel: 947 226239

NOSTRUS
Ctra. Santander, km. 2
Tel: 947 245033

NUMANCIA
Trujillo, 8
Tel: 947 237498

ORTEGA
Mérida, 4
Tel: 947 220836

OSLO
Vitoria, 111
Tel: 947 243162

PALACIO DE LOS
BLASONES
Fernán González, 6-10
Tel: 947 257680

PANCHO
San Lorenzo, 13
Tel: 947 203405

PATATÍN
Avda. Castilla y León,
C.C. Camino de la Plata, L.17
Tel: 947 228059

PARDO
Pza. Antonio José, 4
Tel: 947 223938

PASCUAL
Diego Polo, 4-6
Tel: 947 274272

POLVORILLA
Pza. de la Libertad, 9
Tel: 947 257474

PUERTA ROMEROS
San Amaro, 2
Tel: 947 460738

PULPERÍA LALÍN A
MORRIÑA
San Isidro, 4 y 6
Tel: 947 273029

PUNTA BRAVA
Villalón, 2
Tel: 947 208211

RIALARES
Avda. de la Constitución
Española, 23
Tel: 947 219638

RICE
Avda. Reyes Católicos, 30
Tel: 947 222300

RINCÓN DE ESPAÑA
Nuño Rasura, 11
Tel: 947 205955

RINCÓN DE LA LLANA
Llana de Adentro, 2
Tel: 947 205917

RINCÓN DE
LA MERCED
Merced, 13
Tel: 947 479900

SALAMANCA
Miranda, 7
Tel: 947 278002

SAN ARNALDUS
Gnral Santocildes, 7
Tel: 947 271997

SOTILLANO
Avellanos, 5
Tel: 947 206188

SUR
Oviedo, 3
Tel: 947 265992

SUSI
Camino Casa la Vega, 35
Tel: 947 208991

TABERNA DE TANÍN
Doctor Fleming, 7
Tel: 947 279999

TABERNA DEL
CORRALÓN
Corral de los Infantes, 3
Tel: 947 205997

TABERNA DEL MAR
Regino Sáiz de la Maza, 5
Tel: 947 272720

TAPELIA
Plaza del Rey San Fernando, s/n
Tel: 947 201574

TEODORO
Avda. del Cid, 65
Tel: 947 221082

TIMOTEO
Vitoria, 217
Tel: 947 483794

TONI Y VITO
Regino Sáiz de la Maza, 9
Tel: 947 272102

TORRES
Vitoria, 228
Tel: 947 210132

TROL
San Lorenzo, 25
Tel: 947 263394

VIENA
Farmaceútico Obdulio Fernández, 36
Tel: 947 227558

VILLADIEGO
Casillas, 9
Tel: 947 266162

VINOTECA CORDÓN
La Puebla, 3
Tel: 947 277279

ZATORRE
Burguense, 24
Tel: 947 265961

INTERNATIONAL CUISINE

BURGER KING
Avda. Castilla y León Centro Comercial Camino de la Plata
Tel: 947 231512

CANTINA TEQUILA
Santa Águeda, 8-10
Tel: 947 209298

CANTINA MARIACHI
C.C. El Mirador, Local 3
Ctra. Santander, km. 2,5
Tel: 947 221800

CHE BOLUDO
Santiago, 50
Tel: 947 225487

CHINA TOWN
Reyes Católicos, 34
Tel: 947 237422

DAO XIAN CHUNG
Avda. del Cid, 59
Tels: 947 232059 / 947 237422

FON-LAI
Avda del Vena, 6
Tel: 947 230006

GRAN MURALLA
Santiago, 2
Tel: 947 237676

HONG-KONG BURGOS
Madrid, 4
Tel: 947 250357

MAC DONALD'S
Ctra. Santander, km 2
Tel: 947 227328

MAC DONALD'S
Parque Burgos, N-I km, 236
Tel: 947 279012

ORIENTAL
San Juan de los Lagos, 8
Tel: 947 230017

PEKÍN
Arzobispo de Castro, 3
Tel: 947 215126

PONTE VECCHIO
Vitoria, 111
Tel: 947 225650

PREGO
Huerto del Rey, 4
Tel: 947 260447

RICHI'S
San Lesmes, 1
Tel: 947 200012

SHANG-HAI
Vitoria, 49
Tel: 947 270394

TABERNA DE TRAGOS LA NEGRA CANDELA
Huerto del Rey, 19
Tel: 947 202844

TAJ-MAHAL
Avda Constitución Española, 3
Tel: 947 236900

THE FOX TAVERN
Espolón, 4
Tel: 947 273311

VEGETARIANO GAIA
Fernán González, 37
Tel: 947 279728

VILLA TRAJANO
Avda. Reyes Católicos 8
Tel: 947 264455

My guide

VILLAGONZALO ARENAS
POLIGONO INDUSTRIAL DE VILLALONQUEJAR
VILLALONQUEJAR
BARRIADA JUAN YAGÜE
VILLALBILLA
FF. CC. Madrid - Irún
BARRIO DEL PILAR
DE LEON
N-120
POLIGONO INDUSTRIAL LOS BREZOS
VILLACIENZO
RENUNCIO
E-80
N-620
VILLAGONZALO - PEDERNALES
DE VALLADOLID